To Jonathan!

With love,

Mother & Daddy —

LIMITING GOD

With my love,

Brett.

By the same author . . .

KNOWING GOD'S SECRETS

LIMITING GOD

An Analysis of Christian Failure
With the Sure Answer for Success

by

JOHN E. HUNTER

ZONDERVAN PUBLISHING HOUSE
Grand Rapids, Michigan

DEDICATED TO MY WIFE
WHOSE ENCOURAGEMENT
AND HELP
HAVE MADE THIS BOOK
POSSIBLE

CONTENTS

LIMITING GOD

Chapter 1

LIMITING GOD FOR US

THE OLD TESTAMENT is the rich and blessed treasure house of God. There is comfort and challenge, light and guidance, teaching and direction in all its pages. It speaks much of things to come, it makes many prophecies and promises, but it finishes with a feeling that "this is not the end!"

The New Testament is the glorious complement of the Old. All the promises and prophecies are either fulfilled in it or given a new meaning. The New Testament simply had to be written to vindicate the faithfulness of a Holy God.

But the New Testament by itself is definitely incomplete. Many times we read, " . . . that the Scriptures might be fulfilled" — words that point back to the promises of God. Characters are referred to and incidents recalled in such a way that without the knowledge of the Old Testament the New Testament could not make complete sense. Each of the Testaments is wonderfully interwoven with the other. There is a family likeness between them. Types are fulfilled, and the most impossible prophecies come true. Through all the writings shines the holy character of the Divine Author.

In I Corinthians 10:1-12 Paul refers to the Old Testament record of God's dealings with the children of Israel on their journey from Egypt to Canaan. As he points to their failings and sins, he links us with them in verses 7-10.

Neither be ye idolaters, as were some of them. . . . Neither let us commit fornication, as some of them committed. . . . Neither let us tempt Christ, as some of them also tempted. . . . Neither murmur ye, as some of them also murmured. . . .

Most certainly the Holy Spirit is challenging us, and to make it more emphatic, He adds in verse 11 — "Now all these things happened unto them for ensamples: and they are written for our admonition. . . ." In other words the Spirit points us back to the Old Testament, especially to the experiences of the children of Israel, saying, "All the things that happened to them are examples, or types, of the way you may behave, and they are written for your admonition, or your warning." As we read their story we will see ourselves today. So let us take warning, lest the consequences of their failure come upon us. If we feel ourselves to be above such weakness, verse 12 tells us, "Wherefore let him that thinketh he standeth take heed lest he fall."

How important this warning must be, in the eyes of the Spirit of God, when He sends it, not to those who are falling in the Christian pathway, but to those who feel they are continuing to stand. In this way God uses the records of the Old Testament as a textbook for *personal* Christian living; He directs His warning to "*him* that thinketh he standeth. . . ."

Never was there a day when such a message was more needed. The personal life of the believer — the overwhelming need for personal purity and victory — is the greatest priority in the Church today. There never was so much evangelistic activity as there is at present. The Church of God seems alive to this need. In so many ways the message of the Gospel is being sent out. In our own land every means is used and exploited. It is comparatively easy to hear the Gospel. But, more and more, I am realizing that evangelism is not enough. I have traveled much, and seen and heard and noticed — and now I am more convinced than ever that behind the message of the Gospel there must be a walk, a life, of personal holiness and purity. The Lord Jesus said that "by their fruits ye shall know them" (Matthew 7:20). We often get taken in by the size of the tree, or the wonderful shapes and colors of the leaves, or the glorious display of floral beauty. The Lord said, "by their *fruits*. . . ."

It is interesting to examine these verses in I Corinthians for Paul's use of pronouns. Sometimes he includes himself as being capable of the specific failure. At other times he points to his readers only as being in danger. In verse 6 he says, "Now these things were our examples, to the intent we should not lust after evil things. . . ." Here Paul includes himself, recognizing his own potential weakness in this area of temptation. In verse 7 he says, "Neither be ye idolaters. . . ." Here he excludes himself. The man who could say, "For me to live is Christ" (Philippians 1:21), could never be guilty of being an idolater.

In the next verse Paul is again very conscious of his own weak flesh: "Neither let us commit fornication [sexual looseness]." And in verse 9 — "Neither let us tempt Christ" — Paul included himself as a possible victim of this sin. In verse 10 he says, "Neither murmur ye," excluding himself. The man who could say, "I have learned, in whatever state I am, therewith to be content" (Philippians 4:11) would never be guilty of grumbling if things went wrong.

Paul sums it all up by saying that all these things are written for our admonition, showing his sense of his own need of the warning. See how this adds much more punch to verse 12: "Wherefore let him that thinketh he standeth take heed lest he fall." Paul had not arrived; he wasn't too big for such a warning. But some of us may be so. We may think our advanced civilization has given us, personally, the answer to moral failure. Not so. It is this kind of thinking Paul warns us about. This is the great message for the church today.

So it is that this message from I Corinthians 10:1-12 comes to us with a sense of urgency. Are we, in our day and generation, following the example of the children of Israel? The word is so plain which tells us that these things happened as types; they are written for our warning.

The purpose of this little book is to take heed to the warning given by God. We will do as we are bidden, and look at the recorded incidents to see if there is a message for us.

In Psalm 78 God uses the same method to teach His people of that generation. He shows them the whole story of the children of Israel from Egypt up to their own time. In verses 4-8 we read —

> We will not hide them from their children . . . that the generation to come might know them . . . that they might set their hope in God, and not forget the works of God, but keep his commandments: and might not be as their fathers, a stubborn and rebellious generation; a generation that set not their heart aright, and whose spirit was not stedfast with God.

The warnings continue right through the seventy-two verses of the psalm. Verse 41 seems to gather together the whole idea and to sum up the effect of Israel's failure: "Yea, they turned back and tempted God, and limited the Holy One of Israel."

What an unusual thought this is — that these people limited God. The Almighty Creator God was limited by the creature. They, of their own free will, shut God up in a wilderness. They pushed God into a corner. It wasn't that God was not strong enough, or powerful enough, but that His people deliberately chose to limit Him.

They limited God in two distinct ways. First they limited what God could do *for* them, and then they limited what God could do *through* them. In Deuteronomy 1:2 we read: "There are eleven days' journey from Horeb by the way of mount Seir unto Kadesh-barnea." But the next verse says, "And it came to pass in the fortieth year." How amazing! Forty years later they had still not reached the land of Canaan! What could have been accomplished in days, was finally completed in over forty years. So the Bible says that "they limited God" — in their progress.

What could and should have been a continuous forward movement — pressing on, counting on God's promise, expecting nothing but blessing — became a failure. Their speed slowed down and eventually they stopped. They ceased progressing and started to wander. They lost their vision of the Promised Land and were content with a much lower standard. Dissatisfaction, disappointment, disaster and disobedience became the accepted norm of their daily life. God was limited.

Further on, in Deuteronomy 6:20-25, we are told what an Israelite had to say to his son if he asked questions —

> Then thou shalt say unto thy son, We were Pharaoh's bondmen in Egypt; . . . and the Lord brought us out from thence, that he might bring us in.

God's purpose was to deliver His people from Egypt, and to bring them into Canaan. There was to be a continuous movement, as it were, out of Egypt right into Canaan. God's intention was to take them from the bondage and suffering of Egypt right into the freedom and riches of Canaan. His redemption was not out of Egypt into the wilderness, but out of Egypt into Canaan.

But again, the Bible says that "they limited God" — not only in their progress but also in their possessions. There was so much more that God could do for them, was willing to do for them, but they of their own free will limited Him. Through their own stupidity, ignorance and disobedience, they insisted on taking their own way. They disregarded all the warnings of a God who loved them and cared for them, whose one desire was to bless them — and so they limited Him.

They possessed nothing, although everything was theirs. All the pastures were theirs, pastures which gave milk and honey. All the hills were theirs, hills which gave the metals they needed. All the cities were theirs, cities which contained the houses and furniture they needed. Everything was theirs, the moment they stepped out of Egypt. All they had to do was to possess their possessions.

As God said to Balaam, (Numbers 22:12) "Thou shalt not curse the people: for they are blessed." They were blessed indeed, but they wouldn't claim their blessing. They accepted defeat as the normal way of life. Because of all this they limited what God could do for them. They made no progress and had no possessions. And the tragedy was that they chose so to be. God could have done so much more, so very much more, but they limited Him and suffered in consequence.

The Word of God in I Corinthians 10:11 has been saying to us that we are to look for types of our own behavior and take a warning. We can realize now with a shock that what the Israelites did is terribly true of many of us. Just as the Word of God summed up their behavior by saying, "They limited God," so it might also sum up Christians' behavior today. Everything we have considered so far can be a type of our own behavior. We, too, have been redeemed from Egypt, from a world which held us in bondage to sin. We have been redeemed by the blood of a lamb — Christ our passover is sacrificed for us (I Corinthians 5:7). As Deuteronomy 6:23 says, God brought us out, that He might bring us in. God's plan for us is a deliverance from a bondage to sin, to a completely new life in Christ Jesus.

We read in II Corinthians 5:17, "Therefore if any man be in Christ, he is a new creature: old things are passed away; behold all things are become new." If I am a true child of God then I am in Christ. In John 17:20, 21, our Lord prayed for us:

Neither pray I for these alone, but for them also which shall believe on me through their word; that they all may be one; as thou, Father, art in me, and I in thee, that they also may be one in us. . . .

If I am a believer on Jesus Christ, then I am in Him, and if I am in Him, I am a new creature — a new creation — old things have passed away, and all things have become new. Notice, this is true of me now according to God's promise: "if any man be in Christ, he *is* a new creature" — not "he will be" but *he is* right now. God brought me out of sin that He might bring me into Christ. He brought you out that He might bring you in.

But so many of us are stuck in the wilderness. All things are ours in Christ but, like the Israelites, we limit God. Just as they limited God in making no progress, many of us are content to have a wilderness type of Christianity. The characteristic word in the wilderness is *wandering*. The children of Israel wandered, sometimes going round in circles. How true this is of some of us, both as individuals and as churches. There can be plenty of activity, much of which at first sight seems good and healthy, but when it is examined for progress in spiritual grace and truth, there is nothing to report. Plenty of leaves, quite a lot of pretty flowers, but no fruit. Why is this so? Simply because we do not go on and make progress.

There is one verse in the Bible which has meant more to me in this respect than any other. It is Colossians 2:6: "As ye have therefore received Christ Jesus the Lord, so walk ye in him." It fits in so well with our present thought of progressing into Christ. "As ye have received . . . so walk." Walking isn't wandering, walking is making progress. Here is the secret of progress: "As ye have received . . . so walk."

When I came as a sinner to Jesus I received Him as my own personal Saviour. I didn't believe an ethic, or join a church, or sign a form. I accepted a Person.

For God so loved the world, that he gave his only begotten Son, that whosoever believeth in him should not perish, but have everlasting life (John 3:16).

God gave a gift — His Son — and I accepted that gift. I received Jesus Christ. Not only did I believe in His work, but I accepted His Person. God's salvation isn't a place or a passage. It is a Person. So Colossians 2:6 tells us, "As ye have received . . . so walk." How did I receive Christ? I received Him by faith and with empty hands. I did nothing toward my salvation — "not by works of righteousness which we have done" (Titus 3:5). I simply realized my need, believed God's answer to my need, and accepted Christ as my Saviour. The moment I accepted Him I was saved, delivered out of Egypt's bondage by the shed blood of Christ. Also, I was in Christ, and because I was in Christ, I became a new creature.

Now that is perfectly true positionally and potentially, but very often it is not true practically. What I failed to do was to go on — to walk as I had received. I thought that because I had received Jesus as my Saviour, that was that. My sins were forgiven, I was saved, so now I had to be a good boy and live the Christian life. But that is where I got stuck in the wilderness, wandering and limiting God. I thought it was up to me now to live a good life, doing my best to serve Him — but nothing ever seemed to happen. I spent many years wandering in the desert. I wasn't in Egypt any more. I had been delivered, but I found it rather miserable, and sometimes monotonous living in the wilderness. Sometimes I came upon a little oasis which was very thrilling, but it only served to make me long for more such places.

Then one day God opened this verse to me. As I had received Christ Jesus, in just the same way I had to walk, day by day, *in Him.* I had to walk *in Him,* not in the wilderness. Jesus Christ is Canaan. God brought me out so that He could bring me in — *in Christ.* Praise God, I had discovered the secret of progress. In His mercy, God let me see the simplicity of the whole thing. I just have to walk, receiving. When I came at first, I received Christ. Now as I walk day by day, I continue to receive Him. He is all I need. He is made unto me all I can ever want.

So now my daily Christian life is a moment by moment experience of receiving Christ. Whatever problem, fear, anxiety, temptation or frustration comes into my life, it isn't my job to meet it. My job is to expose the whole situation to Christ Jesus the Lord, and then to walk believing that what He has promised He will also perform.

This is what God means when He says in II Corinthians 5:17 that "old things are passed away; behold, all things are become new." So many of us are positionally and potentially new creatures in Christ, but practically we are still doing the old things, still wandering in the wilderness and getting nowhere. But all things can become new if only we will walk day by day, moment by moment, receiving "all that He is, for all that I need."

Earlier in this chapter we spoke of the need, not for increased evangelism, but for the life behind the message. The greatest need in the church of God today is that those who profess and call themselves Christians should have a life which backs up the message. "As he which hath called you is holy, so be ye holy in all manner of conversation" (I Peter 1:15). When we remember that the word "conversation" means "conduct and manner of living" we find ourselves back to Colossians 2:6: "As ye have therefore received Christ Jesus the Lord, so walk ye in him."

It is essential that my life should be pure and holy — essential, not optional. If I allow sin, failure, defeat and any other of the "old things" to dominate in my daily walk, then I am limiting God from beginning to end. If I go on doing this in spite of His warning, I will make a farce of my Christian walk, a fool of myself and a friend of the devil.

We have been thinking in this chapter of the tragedy of limiting God in what He can do for us. We have considered Deuteronomy 6:23 where it is recorded that God "brought us out . . . that he might bring us in." Verse 24 goes on to say: "And the Lord commanded us to do all these statutes . . . for our good always." The whole plan and purpose of God is "for our good always." God never limits His blessings to us. The measure of God's unlimited desire to give is recorded for us in Malachi 3:10:

> Bring ye all the tithes into the storehouse . . . prove me now herewith, saith the Lord of hosts, if I will not open you the windows of heaven, and pour you out a blessing, that there shall not be room enough to receive it.

How God longs to give! Listen to God's longings for us recorded in Deuteronomy 5:29:

> O that there were such an heart in them, that they would fear me, and keep all my commandments always, that it might be well with them, and with their children for ever!

The tragedy of missing the blessing, of limiting God's goodness, is that it comes through our own disobedience.

CHAPTER 2

LIMITING GOD THROUGH US

IN THE LAST CHAPTER we considered Psalm 78:41, where the Lord sums up the ways of the children of Israel in these words, "they . . . limited the Holy One of Israel." We thought of this as a twofold limitation: they limited what God could do *for* them and they also limited what God could do *through* them. Our main concern then was with the idea of limiting what God can do for us. In this chapter we want to think of how we limit what God can do through us.

We need first of all to get our priorities right. If God is limited in what He can do for you, then most certainly He will be limited in what He can do through you. It was this way with the children of Israel. God could have done so much more, humanly speaking, if He had had the full co-operation of His people. Not only would they have been blessed as a people, but they themselves could have been a bigger blessing to all around. We find that, even when they entered Canaan, instead of being a glorious pure witness to Jehovah they became followers of the gods of the dwellers in the land.

In our lives this can be true, too. If we are reflecting the joyous blessing of the presence of Christ, then through us, God can bring blessing to others. His work will be unhindered because of our positive enjoyment of Christ. If, on

21

the other hand, we are living in our own private wilderness, thoroughly miserable and utterly discontented, no one is going to be impressed by the goodness of God. To them He will appear very undesirable, all because of our wilderness behavior. We will have limited God working through us because we have limited what God can do for us.

Psalm 78:9 records the way in which God was limited: "The children of Ephraim, being armed, and carrying bows, turned back in the day of battle." Verse 41 says, "Yea, they turned back. . . ." Verse 57 says again, "but [they] turned back." Three times it is recorded that they turned back. Notice who turned back — it was the children of Ephraim. Ephraim means "twice fruitful" — in other words, those who had been a great blessing on previous occasions. These were not a bunch of useless beggars, but those who had a great record of previous service.

Following our instructions from I Corinthians 10:11, if we look for examples to instruct us today, the word becomes doubly serious. Here are those who have proved themselves in God's service, those, in one sense, on whom God relies. Could this be any of us who seek to serve whether in a large way or a small way?

See also *when* they turned back — right in the day of battle. There had been all the talking, all the planning, all the preparation. Then the great day arrived, and just at the critical moment they turned back. No wonder God was limited in what He could do through them. No wonder the words come three times, "Yea, they turned back." It wasn't because they were weak or ill prepared; verse 9 says they were armed and carrying bows. They had a full equipment for offense and defense. In spite of this, they turned back. They had all the promises of God guaranteeing them His presence and His power, but they still turned back. So they limited God in what He could do through them.

Psalm 78:57 says: "But [they] turned back, and dealt unfaithfully like their fathers: they were turned aside like a deceitful bow." The words "deceitful bow" really mean a "slack bow." The children of Israel were just like a bow for shooting arrows. All the pieces were there — the wooden upright which gave the tension, the string that thrust forth the arrow — but the whole thing was slack. The string hung limp and useless and the bow was utterly ineffective.

A slack bow has, first of all, *no power*. The normal bow in actual use releases the arrow with a "ping," but a slack bow has no power. The arrow just goes plop! and falls to the ground. Secondly, a slack bow has *no purpose*. The normal bow sends the arrow on a true course, but a slack bow has no ability to keep to its purpose. The arrow flies on a wrong course, and the whole action is a failure. Thirdly, a slack bow gives *no pleasure*. Who would want to use a bow which had no power and no purpose. The whole thing is unsatisfactory, and the archer soon puts the slack bow to one side, finding no pleasure in such an object.

The Bible says to us that some of us are like slack bows. We could be so effective in the hands of God if we were not so weak and useless. Slackness in prayer and Bible reading always results in a slack bow — and a slack bow limits God. Remember, too, that "backsliding" comes from "slack-abiding."

But we were thinking of those who were armed yet turned back in the day of battle. How does this apply to us? Are we armed in the day of battle? I John 4:4 contains a precious promise: "Greater is he that is in you, than he that is in the world." Here is something clear, precise and definite. Notice first the "Person" — "greater is he that is in you. . . ." My defense is not my skill nor my studies, but my Saviour — a Person. I John 5:11, 12 tells us quite definitely,

> And this is the record, that God hath given to us eternal life, and this life is in his Son. He that hath the Son hath life; and he that hath not the Son of God hath not life.

God's word teaches us that we are indwelt by the Holy Spirit, the Spirit of Jesus Christ. Romans 8:9 is so sure, "Now if any man have not the Spirit of Christ, he is none of his." If I declare that Jesus does not live in me, then I cut myself off from all God's blessings, for I am none of His. Ephesians 2:12 assures me then that I am without God, without Christ and without hope. But, if I recognize the glorious truth that Jesus Christ dwells in me, in the power and person of His Holy Spirit, then my whole world is changed. Then I can say, the One who is in me is greater.

Notice secondly the power. *"Greater is he that is in you than he that is in the world."* Ephesians 6:11, 12 calls us to arm ourselves because,

> we wrestle not against flesh and blood, but against principalities, against powers, against the rulers of the darkness of this world, against spiritual wickedness in high places.

Your real enemy is not yourself, or your boss, or your competitor, or your neighbor — or Communism! Your real enemy is the prince of this world, the devil. Three times our Lord gave him that title — in John 12:31, 14:30 and 16:11. In Ephesians 2:2 he is called "the prince of the power of the air, the spirit that now worketh in the children of disobedience." He is the power behind the Kremlin . . . "the whole world lieth in the evil one" (I John 5:19, ASV). But we rejoice that the One who indwells us is greater than all the power of the enemy. He said, "All power is given unto me in heaven and in earth . . . and, lo, I am with you alway" (Matthew 28:18-20).

Notice, thirdly, the present tense. "Greater *is* he." I have who I need, what I need — *when* I need. Right now, in the arena of the everyday, in the common things of life I am armed. I John 4:17 tells us that "as he is, so are we in this world." "As he is," — not as he was or will be. I can stand now, armed in all the mighty power of Jesus Christ, with all His capacity for victory, with all His capability to overcome. All this is mine now.

How much more armed are we today than the children of Ephraim were in their day. Well may we agree with Paul. "Thanks be to God, which giveth us the victory through our Lord Jesus Christ" (I Corinthians 15:57). And yet, we limit God. We, too, turn back in the day of battle, although we are so perfectly armed. Why did they turn back? It wasn't lack of power, for God was on their side. It was just fear. Time and again we read that "they were afraid." God could have done so much more, humanly speaking, if His people hadn't been so fearful. His power could have been demonstrated, His glory uplifted, His will displayed. But they limited God through fear.

Here we see probably the greatest cause of our failure — we, too, are afraid. We repeat the text, *"greater is he that is in you, than he that is in the world,"* and then we go and repeat the failure.

Here and there, however, in all ages and in all places, God has had His faithful few. There are men and women who have dared to believe that God meant what He said. They stand out like jewels amid the dust of defeat. It wasn't education that gave them their victory, or ability that took them to triumph, but an absolute faith in an all-powerful God who will always vindicate His promises.

In the world of boxing, a defeated man is often called a horizontal boxer, because of his ultimate position — flat on his back. The greatest weakness of the Christian church at the present time is the quality of our living. There are too many horizontal Christians. The word of God repeatedly calls for us to "stand." Our faith should be vertical, not horizontal. But so many Christians spend their lives picking themselves up off the floor. They get up to struggle a little more, and then down they go in defeat once again. Sad as it may seem, this is the only life some Christians ever know. And so they come to accept a succession of failures and defeats as the "normal" way of living. How can such a Christian serve God? How can he ever become a conqueror when he is always a casualty? No wonder God is limited.

The answer to this shameful situation is a better understanding of God's salvation. If we turn to Romans 5:8 we read that, *"God commendeth his love toward us, in that, while we were yet sinners, Christ died for us."* Notice the past tense in these words. The whole question of my sin has been dealt with. My sins are gone, as we read in Hebrews 10:17: "their sins and iniquities will I remember no more." Hebrews 10:14 says, "For by one offering he hath perfected for ever them that are sanctified."

For many of God's people, however, this is all they know of God's salvation — that their sins are forgiven. Like the little children in I John 2:12 ". . . your sins are forgiven you for his name's sake." But notice that God never washes us from our sins to leave us in our nakedness. God's word says that we are justified (Romans 5:9). To be justified means not only that my sins are washed away, but that I am clothed in the righteousness of Christ. Sometimes a preacher will say that to be justified means to be made "just-as-if-I'd never sinned." Such an explanation is very clever, but is not really correct. Justification means that I am cleansed, then clothed.

In these days of much evangelism, there is some preaching which falls short of the true word of God. A message which is only "Come to Jesus and have your sins forgiven" is insufficient in content, and incomplete in outlook. Such a message may be used to get quick results and bigger figures, but it will surely produce quicker retreats and bigger failures. Inquirers who are assured that by believing in Jesus their sins are forgiven, and are then sent on their way to live for Jesus, are surely heading for defeat. There is more in God's salvation than having my sins forgiven — much more.

The words that follow Romans 5:8 with its past tense, are "Much more then, being now justified by his blood, we shall be saved from wrath through him." Here is the future tense of my salvation — "we shall be saved." Saved from wrath — there will be no Great White Throne judgment for me. I have a past tense to my salvation and a future tense. This aspect of salvation is called being reconciled to God, to have peace with God through our Lord Jesus Christ. (Notice that we are reconciled to God — God is never reconciled to us. We are the guilty party, and we need to be reconciled.)

It would be fairly safe to say that this is what many Christians take as the scope of their salvation. Their sins are forgiven, they have a home in heaven — praise God, how wonderful it is! But just at this point there creeps in the one thing that limits God. The believer, rejoicing in the knowledge of sins forgiven and a home in heaven, now sets out to do the greatest job of his life — to live for Jesus.

I was like that. I was so grateful to my Saviour for my wonderful salvation that I set out to prove my love by living for Him. I rolled up my sleeves and began the great battle of my life. I was going to do great things for Him. I was going to fight, to press on, to suffer, to struggle — all for His sake. As I met defeat and disaster I turned over new leaves, and started again in the battle for Jesus.

Many of God's dear people today are engaged in that fight. If they suffer, then they are glad to pay a price for Him. It sounds so heroic, to fight for Jesus, to win through for Him. But it is so frustrating. The whole tragedy is that we are limiting God. There is more to my salvation than knowing my sins are forgiven and having a home in heaven. There is much more than being reconciled to God. God's word says so!

> For if, when we were enemies, we were reconciled to God by the death of his Son, much more, being reconciled, we shall be saved by his life.

How unusual that sounds. If I asked you how you were saved, you would most probably reply, "I was saved by the death of Christ." Yet in this verse we read that *"we shall be saved by his life."* Is this a contradiction? The answer is that the phrase in the King James version, "we shall be saved by his life," fails to give the real meaning of the original Greek. It fails both in the verb and in the tense. A more helpful translation is that given in the Amplified New Testament, which transforms the whole meaning. "We shall be saved [daily delivered from sin's dominion] through His [resurrection] life." The whole idea now radiates power. I see now the answer to my struggles, to my fears, to my defeat. God's salvation has a present tense. Not only has it a past tense of sins dealt with and a future tense of a home in heaven, but — what I need most of all — a present tense in my daily living.

A few months ago I was counseling Jim, a young man of about nineteen. He came with a heartbroken cry. His great desire was to be a missionary but, he said, "it's no use, I must give up the whole idea, I know my sins are forgiven, and I know I have a home in heaven, but, quite honestly, that isn't my biggest problem. It is nice to know my sins are gone — for that is all settled in Christ. It is good to know I have a home in heaven — but that may be years ahead. My big problem is not the past, or the future, but the present. Can Jesus Christ do anything for me now?"

He then went on to explain how the devil was bringing bitter and evil temptation to him. Even when he was in prayer and meditation, lustful and wicked thoughts, ideas and pictures came into his mind. He told me how he had struggled to remove the foulness. He had made promises, prayed and turned over new leaves, but nothing seemed to give him victory. In an agony he cried, "Oh, how can I find deliverance from this sin?"

We prayed together and turned to God's Word for help and wisdom. First I showed him that temptation is not a sin. That gave him some relief. (How the devil tries to crush the witness and steal the joy of Christians. If the devil can get us to believe that it is a sin to be tempted, then he has already won half the battle.) We looked at the temptations of our Lord, and saw how bitterly He was tempted — not three times only, as some would believe, but, as we read in Luke 4:13 (Amplied New Testament):

> And when the devil had ended every [the complete cycle of] temptation, he left Him — temporarily, that is, stood off from Him until another more opportune *and* favorable time.

The devil was ever seeking to tempt our Lord, but we read in Hebrews 4:15 that He "was in all points tempted like as we are, yet without sin." How important are the words, *in all points . . . yet without sin*.

Having learned that to be tempted is not in itself a sin, we turned then to the translation from Romans 5:10, *"daily delivered from sin's dominion by His resurrection life."* I explained to Jim that the very thing he longed for had already been provided. He could be daily delivered from sin's dominion, from the lustful temptations the devil brought to his mind. This deliverance came through the resurrection life of Christ. We considered the thoughts mentioned earlier in this chapter — that Jesus Christ lives in the believer in the Person and power of His Holy Spirit.

Jim's problem now was to find out how the indwelling Christ could help him overcome the temptations of the enemy. I suggested to Him that he should imagine that the center of his conscious mind was like a television screen. On this screen was flashed each thought and idea as it was held in his attention. The form of the devil's attack was to flash on the screen lustful and impure thoughts and ideas. Even while Jim might be in prayer, on that screen came the attack of the enemy. Jim's attempts to remove the thoughts had only served to help bring them back again. By focusing his attention on them he had linked them to his own thought sequence. The way to remove these temptations was not to grapple with them in deadly combat — that would only play into the hands of the devil. The sure way to win was to put something better and stronger in their place.

We then turned to the word of God and found the wonderful words in I Corinthians 15:57: "But thanks be to God, which giveth us the victory through our Lord Jesus Christ." Here was the answer to Jim's problem — victory now through our Lord Jesus Christ. Every time the enemy swept in to the attack Jim was to say with conscious deliberation, "Thank You, Lord Jesus, You are my victory." It might require much repetition at first. He would have to stand firm and claim the victory in Christ.

That is what Jim did. I spoke to him at intervals over the following weeks and found out the result. He said that at first it was a hard fight, just claiming the victory, just saying "Thank You, Lord Jesus, You are my victory." It took maybe twenty or thirty repetitions to cleanse his "screen." As the days went by the victory came quicker because, very soon, the entrance of a foul thought immediately triggered off the prayer of victory.

What Jim was doing was putting into practice God's answer to all the dominion of sin. He was claiming a victory which had already been won, instead of fighting a battle which had already been lost.

This is the only successful answer to all the problems that come our way. We considered earlier in the chapter the glorious promise in I John 4:4, *"Greater is he that is in you than he that is in the world."* The indwelling Christ is our armor. We saw, too, how so many Christians are limiting what God can do through them because of personal defeat in their own lives. This, above all else, is the weakness of the church today — the personal weakness and defeat of each member. If we could come, like Jim did, in all our weakness, and claim personal and daily victory — "Thank You, Lord Jesus, You are my victory" — what a different story it would be. The limiting of God would disappear as the reality of the indwelling presence and power of Christ was manifested.

Someone may say, "Yes, but I don't get temptations like Jim did. I'm older and the lusts of the flesh are not so strong." The thing to realize is that sin is not only vileness of the flesh in drunkenness and sexuality. The most searching definition of sin is found in Romans 14:23: "for whatsoever is not of faith is sin."

Whatsoever is not of faith — this is a searching phrase. The one who isn't attacked by lust will be sure to have other problems looming up against him. *Whatsoever is not of faith* — this puts care, fear, anxiety, worry as weapons in the hand of the devil. How many Christians are snarled up by worry and anxiety! If we could only realize that we can be daily delivered from this kind of dominion, how much more joyous would be our lives. The word of God is firm and sure that we can be daily delivered from sin's dominion by Christ's resurrection life.

I wonder if these words are being read by an anxious mother who doesn't know where to turn. God's salvation has a present tense for you. You can be delivered, moment by moment, if you will claim the victory of Christ. Dare you put Him to the test and cry in all sincerity, "Thank You, Lord Jesus. You are my Victory, You are my Peace"? It is for you. He has promised, "I will never leave thee nor forsake thee." Why not claim a victory which has already been won instead of fighting the battle which you know is lost, even before you begin?

Are these words being read by a man who is beset with the problems of business? Whether it is success or failure, each brings a tension that stretches out the nerves in a fever of spontaneous anxiety. Is your physical health beginning to suffer? Is your family life beginning to crack? Is your church life a burden? There is sure peace for you in the present tense of God's salvation. In spite of all you have done and cannot do, "Greater is he that is in you than he that is in the world." If you would only relate your problem to the victorious Christ; if you would take all that He is for all that you need, you could move into a present-tense experience of the peace of God that passes all understanding. Quit the fight and claim the victory.

Much of my work is with teenagers and young adults. It is heartbreaking at times to see those who could be wonderful weapons in the hands of God, lying idle and tied up with personal failure and present defeat. I wonder, are these words being read by some young woman or young man. You have trusted Christ as your Saviour and you know you are saved, but like Jim, you are paralyzed by repeated failure, and desperate through defeat in your personal life. Is it any comfort to you to know that you are not the only one in such a plight?

Many young people have an area in their lives where they know nothing but failure. Many a young man or woman is defeated by a secret habit of thought or word or deed. No one knows but you; you dare not tell anyone. How hard you have struggled and fought against it. Perhaps you started to play with sin some time ago, but now you are caught in its power. The whole thought of this acts as a sickening drag on your own personal life for Christ. There is so much more you want to do, but because of your secret sin you wouldn't dare. Suppose they found you out, you would never show your face again. There are hundreds of young men and women who are limiting God because of personal defeat in their lives. The devil knows it and he wants to keep you there. He has lost you from his kingdom, but if he can paralyze your witness for Christ, he has neutralized your effectiveness as a child of God.

Why don't you stand in the armor of God? Get on your knees first of all, before your Saviour. Tell Him all the story of miserable defeat. Turn from your failure. Trust in Christ for a present tense salvation, then claim the victory that Christ has already won for you. "Thank You, Lord Jesus, You are my Victory." Keep on thanking Him for it. Dare to take Him at His word. Go on to grow strong in the Lord of Hosts, and in His mighty power. Prove to the devil and yourself that "greater is he that is in you than he that is in the world." Stop fighting a battle which has already been lost, and go on to claim the Victory which has already been won — His Victory. Make it yours.

Paul says in Romans 7:18: "I know that in me (that is, in my flesh,) dwelleth no good thing." In II Timothy 1:12 he cries:

> I know whom I have believed, and am persuaded that he is able to keep that which I have committed unto him against that day.

Two things he knew — first his own utter degradation, secondly the overwhelming supremacy of the One to whom he had committed all. Thus he affirms in Philippians 4:13: "I can do all things through Christ which strengtheneth me." The Amplified New Testament has it:

> I have strength for all things in Christ Who empowers me — I am ready for anything and equal to anything through Him Who infuses inner strength into me [that is, I am self-sufficient in Christ's sufficiency].

Does that make you hungry for such an experience? And yet what did Paul have that you don't? Paul had Christ indwelling him and so have you. The great difference is that,

in Paul, Christ had a willing weapon — God wasn't limited
in Paul. God need not be limited in your life if only you will
commit to Him every area of your personality. Paul said that
Jesus Christ was "able to keep that which I have committed
unto him." He keeps what I commit — it is as simple as that.
He keeps what I commit. If I will commit to Him every area
of my life, my areas of defeat as well as my areas of success,
then He can move in and live through me.

Some of us hide our shame. We feel that Jesus Christ
could never use such an abject failure as we are. We long
for a greater experience of effectiveness in His service, but
one glance at our life is sufficient to discourage us. We gaze
on our areas of shame and failure, we hang our heads in
sorrow — and we limit God. Listen again to Paul speaking:
"I have strength for all things in Christ who empowers me."
You, too, can claim that strength to conquer in the place
of defeat. The strength is in Christ who can empower you.
Go forward in faith claiming the victory. Say, "Lord Jesus,
this is my area of defeat, this is my place of shame (declare
it openly to your Lord). Now, O blessed Master, I commit
this to You. I commit my failure, my struggles, my tears. I
claim Your victory. I believe that You have won the victory,
therefore I claim Your victory. Thank You, Lord Jesus. You
are my victory!"

Live in the good of the present tense of your salvation:
"daily delivered from sin's dominion by his resurrection life."

A further meaning to Paul's statement in Philippians 4:13
is, "I am ready for anything and equal to anything through
Him Who infuses inner strength into me." When you have
claimed the victory and proved the victory in your place of
defeat, then you, too, can go on to say, "I am ready for anything and equal to anything, through Him Who infuses inner
strength into me." Like blind Bartimeus, you can throw away
your garment (your rags of shameful defeat), and go on to be

a weapon in the hands of God. You will cease to limit God because you will be completely available and utterly expendable in His hands.

Before Paul could go on to do all things through Christ, he had to see his own utter failure and ruin and degradation. He had to see it, to admit it, to acknowledge it and then to turn from it. Freely admitting that he had not one shred of goodness, he turned from all his failure to all the sufficiency of Christ.

In your life, and my life, this twofold act is essential for blessing. We, too, must recognize the utter worthlessness of our fallen human nature. Then we must turn from it to receive the fullness of the indwelling Christ — "all that He is for all that I need."

CHAPTER 3

LIMITING GOD THROUGH SELFISHNESS

IF WE READ PSALM 78 again, we find two things standing out clearly. All the way through the psalm we meet the loving kindness of God to His people. The goodness of God is revealed again and again. Verse 4 recalls the praises of the Lord — His strength — His wonderful works. Verse 12 introduces the marvellous things He did "in the sight of their fathers." Then the psalmist lists them: He divided the sea. He clave the rocks in the wilderness. He brought streams out of the rock. He rained down manna to eat. He rained flesh upon them as dust. He being full of compassion, forgave their iniquity. The psalm closes with these lovely words, "So He fed them according to the integrity of his heart; and guided them by the skilfulness of His hands." The whole psalm is a graphic record of the goodness of God poured out upon His people.

Over against this grace of God is recorded the mean ingratitude of those He had redeemed. The psalmist lists their behavior starting with verse 10: They kept not the covenant of God, and refused to walk in His law. They forgot His works. They spoke against God; they said, "Can God furnish a table in the wilderness? . . . Can He give bread also? can He provide flesh for His people?" For all this they sinned still, and believed not for His wondrous works. Verses 34 and 36 show how double-hearted they were:

When he slew them, then they sought him: and they returned and enquired early after God. . . . Nevertheless they did flatter him with their mouth, and they lied unto him with their tongues.

The utter selfishness and meanness of the people comes to us almost as a physical blow. God gave them nothing but love, and they spurned the hand that fed them. Even their seeming words of thanks were only flattery and lies. How our spirits rise in condemnation of such ingratitude.

But let us look at the way these people behaved in the light of I Corinthians 10, and perhaps we will see types of our own behavior. As we take these words to our hearts each of us is bound to see the pointing finger, and to hear the solemn words, "Thou art the man."

In Ephesians 1:10 we are introduced to the great and wonderful person of Christ and in verse 11 we read that "we have obtained an inheritance" in Him. My inheritance is Jesus Christ. The very words open up the thought of the rich goodness of God towards us. Our sins have been cleansed in Christ's precious blood. We have been brought near to God in Him. We have been accepted by God in Him. Jesus Christ is my Redeemer, my Saviour, my Advocate. He is the source of all the love and joy and peace in my life. All this we know and all this we take.

But the other side of the picture is in verse 18:

The eyes of your understanding being enlightened; that ye may know what is the hope of his calling, and what the riches of the glory of his inheritance in the saints.

Here is Christ's inheritance in us. In other words, just as I cannot function without all that He is, so, in an amazing way, He cannot fulfill His true purposes without all that I am. We are His inheritance, His tools, His weapons, the vehicles He uses to implement His own will.

At this point, perhaps, we can see ourselves in the types of Psalm 78. The children of Israel took all God offered. They asked for more, they expected more, they demanded more, and God gave freely for their needs. But God got very little in return. They were selfish, base, mean, full of ingratitude. They limited God through their selfishness. Can this be true of some of us? Do we take so willingly all our inheritance in Christ? We expect to be blessed, comforted and forgiven. We hold Him to His promises and say almost like Jacob in Genesis 32:26, "I will not let Thee go, except Thou bless me." We demand our rights — and God honors His word and pours out His patient grace.

But if the Lord comes to us, and seeks for His inheritance in us — that is a different story. We don't mind taking all that He gives, but we are bitterly slow to respond to His request. He created us, He redeemed us, we are not our own but He has bought us with a price — all this we agree to in principle. But if the Lord needs us and calls for us, we reply, "Behold, here am I, send someone else."

God is shamefully limited by the selfishness of His people. Every cent you own is His. Every second you live is His. Every breath you draw is in His hands. But in one way and another we beg to be excused. We have just one short life in which we can serve Him before we spend an eternity enjoying the "much more" of our glorious inheritance in Him, only one short life to prove our love, to begin to respond to the agony of Olivet and the suffering of Calvary. But time and again we say, "I pray Thee have me excused."

In our response to Christ we are far worse than ever the children of Israel were in the desert. We withhold our finances, our fellowship, our fruitfulness — and God's work is limited. We talk about "my money," "my time," "my life," as if these were our prize possessions, as if we could do with them as we would.

There is a very searching word in Psalm 12:1 — "Help, Lord, for the godly man ceaseth; for the faithful fail from among the children of men." How crisp is the phrasing, *the ceasing of the godly,* the *failing of the faithful.* Usually the psalmist deals with the harm done by the wicked in their opposition to the ungodly, but here the cry is against the godly and the faithful. Those who were godly are now ceasing, those who were faithful are now failing.

Verse 4 of the same psalm tells us why the godly are ceasing and the faithful failing: "Who have said, With our tongue will we prevail; our lips are our own: who is lord over us?" How modern is their reply, "My lips are my own, who is Lord over me?" People say today, "My time is my own, my money is my own, who is going to tell me what to do?" This is the selfishness that limits God — when the child of God denies to Jesus Christ the inheritance for which He died.

We read in Hebrews 12:2 that Jesus Christ "for the joy that was set before him endured the cross, despising the shame." Part of that joy was His inheritance in the saints, His inheritance in you and me. How pathetic to think that our response to the love of Calvary is the selfishness of a heart that keeps back what it doesn't possess, and holds on to what belongs to another.

As I am writing this now, it is Christmas Eve. Everywhere are the sights and sounds of Christmas. If we forget the commercialization of the festival for a moment, there still remains so much that is lovely and precious. The sweet fragrance of Christmas can still be felt within the hearts of faithful believers. The message of Christmas is being sung again — "Glory to God in the highest, on earth peace." These are the two things the coming of Christ effected — glory to God and peace on earth.

There can be no doubt that the coming of Christ brought glory to God. The angels said it would, the Father openly declared His good pleasure in His Son, and the Lord Himself in John 17:4 pronounced the fact, "I have glorified thee on the earth." These words, coming at the end of the earthly life that started in Bethlehem, give a full and authentic verdict — "I have glorified thee on the earth."

There is no doubt of the glory — but to talk of peace on earth is another matter entirely. With the world split into two armed camps, the idea of peace on earth seems a sheer impossibility. The cruel, cold facts reported daily by newspapers, TV and radio sicken the hearts of all who long for peace. Descending from the international level, through the national, through the domestic and family level, to the individual, the absence of peace everywhere is a stark reality. We are told that the ordinary man and woman of every country, every race, longs for one thing only — peace. But the peace so desired seems further away than ever this Christmas.

Does this mean that Jesus has failed, that while He could produce the glory, He couldn't produce the peace? No, the answer is still the same as it was in Bethlehem, *"There was no room for them in the inn."* There is still no room for a Saviour, who is Christ the Lord. There is room for a teacher, for a heroic example, for a pattern man, for all the other humanist descriptions applied to the Babe. But to *a Saviour who is Christ the Lord* the world still closes its doors. In this way the world today is limiting God. By locking the door against the Prince of Peace, the fact of peace is locked out also.

The boastful ones may try to persuade themselves that they have peace, like the man in Deuteronomy 29:19, who blesses "himself in his heart, saying, I shall have peace, though I walk in the imagination of mine heart, to add drunkenness to thirst." What a pathetic attitude — he refuses the blessing of God and blesses himself. He assures himself that he will have peace in spite of selfishness and drunkenness. This is the world in which many an unbeliever is living today, a fantastic world built in the imagination, based on the blessing of a drunkard! No wonder God is shut out and limited.

But there is a vital message here for the child of God. Many Christians have no real peace of heart, in spite of the fact that the Lord Jesus came to bring peace. Here again is where the limiting of God is seen. Because these Christians have no real peace themselves, they cannot be the blessing they ought to be. Because God is limited for them, He is limited through them. The finest advertisement God has is a life which is full of peace despite the presence of sorrow, suffering and want.

We have been thinking of how we limit God through selfishness. Selfishness always produces an absence of peace. Show me a person who is enjoying the real, deep peace of God, and you will be showing me someone who is unselfish in thought and word and deed.

At Bethlehem the only place offered was a manger, away from the inn and the fellowship of men. Because they put Him in the manger, nobody in the inn was disturbed or put out of their own room — everyone carried on as before. Because they put Him in the manger, nobody saw Him, except those who came seeking Him. The story of the manger makes a very pretty picture; it can be made to look so lovely and artistic. It may be a lovely picture, but it is a very poor practice. The story of the manger is repeated in many Christian hearts. They have heard the Gospel, the call of God to receive the Lord Jesus. They have opened their hearts to receive Him, but there has been no room in the inn. He has been guided to the manger of the heart, to the outside place.

It is so easy to invite the Lord in and put Him in the manger. There, just as at Bethlehem, no one in the inn is disturbed, nobody is put out of their room, everyone can carry on as before — "business as usual." If He is in the manger no one in the inn will be annoyed, no complaints will be heard. Best of all, if He is in the manger then no one will see Him. He will be on the premises but not in possession; on the site but not in sight. No wonder there is so little peace in many a Christian heart today! No wonder God is so terribly limited! Where there is no presence, there can be no power, no peace.

We saw in Ephesians 1:18 that the Lord Jesus has an inheritance in His people. He has an inheritance in you and in me, but it is not the manger of our hearts. The angel said to Zacharias in Luke 1:17 that his son-to-be would "make ready a people prepared for the Lord." That is exactly what true Christians should be, people prepared for *the Lord*. The angel said to the shepherds in Luke 2:11, "For unto you is born this day in the city of David a Saviour, which is Christ *the Lord*." The angels knew Him for who He really was — the Lord.

The wise men (Matthew 2) knew where to look for a king. They went to a palace to search for a throne. Instead they were sent to an inn to search for a manger. A Lord or King does not live in a manger, he sits on a throne. You cannot rule from a stable, you can only reign on a throne. This seems so obvious and simple, yet how many Christians have put the King in the manger! We, in the United States, do not believe in kings and lords. Our government is a so-called true democracy. The man who rules is an elected representative from the people. There are many Christians who treat their spiritual life as a democracy. They have no kings or lords. The man in charge is an elected representative and very often they themselves are the successful candidate. But Christianity isn't a democracy, it is a dictatorship! There is one Lord only, the Lord Jesus Christ. If He is not Lord of all my life, then He is not Lord at all in my life. If He is in the manger, He cannot be on the throne. If Christ is in the manger, then God is limited.

Why do we repeat the Bethlehem story in our own lives, turning Him away from the inn and leaving Him in the manger? The answer is very simple — because of selfishness. If Christ is kept in the manger it is because we do not wish to disturb the other guests in the inn. The inn of your heart is the place of everyday living, the place where people come and go and where all life's business is transacted. If the Lord came in to take possession, what a disturbance there would be.

The human heart is composed of three parts. My mind, my emotions and my will are the content of my heart or personality. In these three areas the Lord seeks to rule from the throne. It is at this point that the costliness of the Christian life becomes the challenge to our innate selfishness.

John the Baptist's mission was to make ready a people prepared for the Lord. When we bring this message to our own hearts we have many decisions to face. If Jesus Christ is to be Lord of my mind, then my mind must be prepared to receive Him. My thinking processes must be pure and holy. Some of the books I possess may need destroying.

This is what happened in Acts 19:18, 19:

> And many that believed came, and confessed, and shewed their deeds. Many of them also which used curious arts brought their books together, and burned them before all men: and they counted the price of them, and found it fifty thousand pieces of silver.

The first thing these people did when they became Christians was to clean up their libraries. It must have been a wonderful witness for all the townspeople to see over $9,000 worth of books going up in smoke.

There is a tremendous amount of debased literature published these days, some of which finds its way into Christian homes. Jesus Christ must be Lord of my library, and what is dirty or doubtful or drivel, should be burned — not given away. It might prove a costly bonfire, but it will help to prepare my mind for the Lord.

We may need to apply II Corinthians 10:5 to our minds:

> Casting down imaginations, and every high thing that exalteth itself against the knowledge of God, and bringing into captivity every thought to the obedience of Christ.

Some of our imaginations and ambitions may need to be cast down. How searching too, is the idea of bringing into captivity every thought to the obedience of Christ — to consider, as it were, the Lord Jesus, in the person and power of His Holy Spirit, examining and censoring every thought that comes into my mind. This will most certainly prepare my mind for the incoming of the Holy and Just One. Purity of mind is a much despised possession today. Yet, if we are not pure in mind, we cannot be pure in heart, and if we are not pure in heart we cannot see God. Certainly if Jesus Christ leaves the manger of my mind to move into the inn, many of the guests and inmates will be disturbed by His presence and will have to go.

If Jesus Christ is to be Lord of my heart, then He must be Lord also of my emotions and affections. It is here that the outward presence of the indwelling Lord should be most demonstrated. My emotions and reactions are many and varied, almost like the keyboard of a piano. From the deep bass of bitter anger to a sweet treble of tender love, I express my reactions to the incidents in my life. But if Jesus Christ were Lord of my emotional life, and sat at the keys, many of my "recital pieces" would remain unplayed. If He were to initiate my reactions to the incidents of life how different would be my behavior. There would be no sudden outbursts of rage or childish temper, no petty jealousy, no mean thoughts or vicious backbiting, no fawning flattery seeking personal advancement. There would be a purity and a holy quality about my emotions that would be outstanding. It would be on this emotional level that the presence of Christ on the throne would be first noticed.

You see, everyone with whom you relate in thought, word or deed is aware of your emotional attitude to them. If you are ruling your own life then you will display your emotions at your own pleasure. Some of your contacts will feel your love and kindness, others will be disregarded, others will incur your anger or displeasure. You will react as you choose, for your own purpose, regardless of the implications. There will develop a pattern of reaction that will be the emotional characteristic of your personality, and everyone will recognize you from that emotional reaction.

But if Christ is given His inheritance in your emotional life, what a change will be seen. First and foremost, He will have an opportunity to display Himself, and in this will be implemented the purpose of your redemption. He will be incarnate in you and thus He will be able to carry on His ancient work of bringing love, hope and comfort to the needy, the hopeless and the lost. As the Lord Jesus is given the control of your emotions so your whole character will change, and people will notice that something has happened to you. Jesus Christ won't be angry with anyone who hurts you — He will say, "Father, forgive them." He won't be bitter against insult, nor will He retaliate when abused. He will not be fearful in danger, nor panic in sudden fear. He won't be consumed with anxiety nor torn with frustration. He will be the peace of God in your heart, as you learn to say, "Lord Jesus, I am resting in You, I am leaving this to You, I am counting on Your promises that never fail." As you say this, and then do what you say, the peace of God will fill your heart.

Christ on the throne of your emotions is the answer to all life's fears. If you do not yield the throne, it is because you think either He cannot or He will not cope with the situation. "Your Christ" is too small or too distant — yet all the time He lives in your heart and He has said, *"All power is given unto me in heaven and in earth. . . . and, lo, I am with you alway, even unto the end of the world"* (Matthew 28:18, 20). Thus there will be seen in you a gradual change of temperament. People will recognize it, wonder, and ask why. All the time Christ will be magnified in you, and His inheritance will be at His disposal.

How strange that what really satisfies Him will also bring peace and joy to your heart. Over years of experience I have come to see that when Christ controls the emotions He also changes the character of the individual, because character is the pattern resulting from continued emotional reaction. I have also seen the Lord change a person's face. I have watched hardness disappear as the love of Christ is displayed.

I was speaking in Scotland recently when I met an old lady over eighty years old. She looked like a real saint and she prayed like an angel. Her face was the picture of loving devotion. Yet until she was fifty years old she was a wicked woman. She told me herself that she had been in jail over a hundred times for drunkenness and disorder. Married at sixteen she had lived in sin, practicing every form of vice and wickedness. Then one day, in despair, after her husband had hanged himself and her only son had been murdered by his wife, she was on her way to put an end to herself by flinging her broken body into the River Clyde. She passed a building from which came the sounds of hymn singing. As a last contact with the world, she went in, sat down at the back and listened. There God spoke to her and Christ met her need. That Sunday night, thirty-seven years ago, she became a new creature in Christ. Today she simply radiates Christ, in thought and word and deed. She who used to display Satan is now the one in whom Christ has full control. Her face has been changed from lust to love, from wickedness to wonderful peace, from sin to serenity.

When Christ is on the throne of my emotions I become the expression of His heart of love. As He daily expresses Himself through my emotions, the color of His presence is diffused throughout my being. His control is evident, His peace is solidly real, His joy is my delight. Unconsciously I will become more Christlike; I cannot help it, because His presence will cleanse, control and conquer.

Paul said (in Galatians 2:20),

> I am crucified with Christ: nevertheless I live; yet not I, but Christ liveth in me: and the life which I now live in the flesh I live by the faith of the Son of God, who loved me and gave himself for me.

We too may come to know the vital truth, "nevertheless I live, yet not I, but Christ liveth in me" — in our emotions. There will be a clarity of emotional response with an absence of mushy sentimentalism. It will be costly but wonderfully satisfying. Even now as you read these words the Holy Spirit may be putting His finger on the emotional strains and stresses in your life. Perhaps you have refused to apologize and have persisted in your pride. Remember that Christ humbled Himself in the days of His flesh, and if He is living in you, He will still want to humble Himself in the days of your flesh. You can always trust Him to do the right thing at the right time. Christ will never abuse your trust, but He will always be Himself. If He can claim His inheritance to the throne of your emotions, that sphere of limitation will vanish, and Christ will be exalted and glorified.

The third sphere where Christ seeks control is in the area of my will, the executive of my human personality. The mind reasons, the emotions react, and the will responds in an act of decision. The will is like the finger on the trigger. Once the will has responded, the decision is made and the trigger is squeezed. Often the will seems unreasonable, impetuous, stupid. We blurt out a remark, then wish with all our hearts we had never said it. We decide on a course of action and then spend months, sometimes years, in an agony of remorse. How often at a trial the accused sobs out, "I never meant to do it. I don't know what made me do it!" But it was done, and the act, the crime, the murder, came because of an uncontrolled act of the will. In the will, more than any other area of the human heart, the selfishness of man is displayed.

It sounds so obviously true to say, "I have a right to my own will!" That is what the world says and expects. But consider the words of the Son of God, He who was rich, by whom all things were made:

> My meat is to do the will of him that sent me (John 4:34).
> I seek not mine own will, but the will of the Father which hath sent me (John 5:30).
> I came down from heaven, not to do mine own will, but the will of him that sent me (John 6:38).
> O my Father, if it be possible, let this cup pass from me: nevertheless not as I will, but as thou wilt (Matthew 26:39).

He possessed all things, but He yielded His will to the One who had sent Him. Under no other conditions could He possibly have said, *"I do always those things that please him"* (John 8:29).

In no other way can we give to God the pleasure He seeks. Only when He is allowed to overrule, reason and guide in the area of my mind, to react to a given situation through the means of my emotions, and to respond by a decision which He has made — only then can Christ come into His inheritance in me. Only then can His life be lived out in terms of my humanity. Only then can I know that I am not limiting God through selfishness.

CHAPTER 4

LIMITING GOD THROUGH FEAR

IN A PREVIOUS CHAPTER we saw how the children of Israel limited God through fear, when they turned back in the day of battle. But there is another kind of fear mentioned in Psalm 78 which is common today — the fear of indecision. This is the fear that holds back from ever setting out on the way to battle. Verse 8 says that the Israelites in the wilderness were "a generation that set not their heart aright, and whose spirit was not stedfast with God." Verse 37 says of them, "their heart was not right with him, neither were they stedfast in his covenant." These verses give us the same two facts: "their hearts were not set aright" — that is, they were not properly prepared; they were not stedfast — that is, they were not faithful to God.

At the very outset of Israel's journey there was weakness. The whole field of future failure was the harvest of an unprepared heart. Their relationship with God was founded on an unprepared heart and a faithless spirit. An old proverb says, "A good start is half the battle." There are some people in our churches who stand, as it were, in a form of relationship to God without any means of being productive for His glory, because there never was a properly prepared heart.

We can see this thought better if we look at Romans 12:1,2:

1 beseech you therefore, brethren, by the mercies of God, that ye present your bodies a living sacrifice, holy, acceptable unto God, which is your reasonable service. And be not conformed to this world: but be ye transformed by the renewing of your mind, that ye may prove what is that good, and acceptable, and perfect, will of God.

"That good, and acceptable, and perfect will of God" — have you always found the will of God good? Have you always found the will of God acceptable? Have you always found it perfect? Many will say, "Decidedly not! Certainly not always good, definitely not always acceptable, and very often not always perfect, at least where I am concerned." This answer means that somehow we have missed out, because we are definitely expected to be able to prove all three characteristics of God's will — good, acceptable and perfect. The reason we miss out is the same fault we saw in Psalm 78:8, 9 — we start our Christian life with an unprepared heart.

I have found it helpful to understand Romans 12: 1, 2, if I underline the word "present" in verse one and then connect it with a line to the words "that ye may prove" in verse 2. The first kernel of truth is, *Present . . . that ye may prove.* The reason so many of God's people complain about God's dealings with them, why so many find the will of God far from good, acceptable and perfect, is that they would like to turn that sentence round. They would like to prove before they present. "If only God would show me His plan for my life," they say. "If only I knew what lies ahead!" But it doesn't work that way. We cannot first prove the will of God and then, if it is to our liking, go on to present our bodies to Him. God's order is *present . . . that ye may prove.*

At this point the fear mentioned at the beginning of the chapter starts to operate. If our hearts are never properly prepared, we enter into the Christian pathway in a slap-happy way, giving an easy assent to certain facts. It would almost seem, in many cases, that the decision to be a Christian was the end in itself. But the decision is not the end, only a means to an end.

The next essential for proving God is a prepared heart and a faithful spirit — and this is where it hurts. If my heart is to be properly prepared for God, the truth of Romans 12:1 must first be real in my life. I must present my whole self as "a living sacrifice, holy, acceptable unto God." Many of God's people have by-passed that challenge. As they started on their pathway and came to this costly decision, it proved too big for them. They were afraid to face up to it. As a result, their lives only limit God. They are seeking to live the Christian life with an unprepared heart. This means that they have set themselves a pattern for all future behavior under similar circumstances. Whenever faced with the challenge of presenting all to Christ, or with the costliness of the Christian life, they will have to hedge round it, wriggle out of it and evade the issue at all costs.

Let us be perfectly honest about this. There are many Christians sitting in our churches at home who ought to be out on the foreign field. God has challenged them in days gone by, but they had already evaded the issue from the start. When they became children of God there came the call to "present your bodies," but they avoided facing up to their relationship to God — their hearts were not properly prepared.

It is no secret now that in this crazy world in which we live, the United States is ready and prepared for the aggressor. Every minute of every hour of every day, there are planes in the air with bombs ready. In Britain the planes are on the runways, with engines warm and crews standing by. There is the maximum amount of possible preparation so that not one second need be lost in an emergency. Please God they may never be needed, but they are ready at a word of command to meet the aggressor.

"Maximum possible preparation" — that is how you and I ought to be in relation to God. Not that when faced with an opportunity of service for Him, we consider it and think about it then and there. But that we have a heart which has been properly prepared right from the start. We have faced Romans 12:1 and on our knees we have come to the only possible decision. From that moment we, too, are "air-borne, fully prepared, awaiting only the word of command." The tragedy is that so many Christians have dodged the issue at the start. They never said "Yes" and they never said "No." There was just a hazy indecision which meant but one thing, an unprepared heart. So, as always, God was limited because they were unprepared.

Let us bring this verse into the open and face up to it, once and for all. "I beseech you therefore, brethren, by the mercies of God, that ye present your bodies a living sacrifice, holy, acceptable unto God, which is your reasonable service." We should first of all realize what it doesn't mean. To present my body a living sacrifice doesn't mean giving a little more to the offering in church. Nor does it mean going to church more often. Nor does it mean being a better man or woman. Neither does it mean going to Bible College, or to the mission field, or becoming a pastor, or a Christian worker. It means exactly what it says.

I must first of all consider the mercies of God to me — how good He has been to me, how He has saved me from a lost eternity, how He has made it possible for me, at the end of this very short earthly life, to be with Him in a place of perfection — a new heaven where there is no hunger, no separation, no pain, no sorrow and no sin. This blessed place will be my home for eternity! How amazing are the mercies of God, when all the time I might have been left in my sin to go to a Christless eternity of separation from God. I should think on these things until, "by the mercies of God" and because of His everlasting goodness, I kneel before Him to say "thank you."

But my feeling of gratitude is such that words are not enough. Instead of speaking, I present myself to God. I present not only my time, my talents, but my very self, with words like this: "O Heavenly Father, my heart is full of gratitude for all Your goodness to me. I am only a poor wretched sinner, and yet You have made me Your child. You have received me into Your family and into Your everlasting Kingdom. Now, O God, I present myself as a living sacrifice to You, for You to use, as and where You will. My heart is prepared, O God, my hands are off my life. I am ready waiting Your command. For Christ's sake. Amen."

If we are honest about the whole thing, this is the only possible decision to make. As Paul puts it, this is "your reasonable service." (How unreasonable some of us are!) Having made that decision, having presented our bodies in one solemn act of dedication, we may arise and go forward with a prepared heart. We are then in a position of permanent availability, so that God can call on us at any time, and under any circumstances. When the opportunity arises for witness or service, the question of what we should do need never arise. We have made a complete, once-for-all presentation of ourselves, and we expect God to take us at our word.

The sacrifice that I present to God — that is my whole self — must have three characteristics. It must be living, holy, acceptable. If I have made this threefold sacrifice, then I will prove the will of God to be threefold — good, acceptable, perfect. The trinity of presentation brings a trinity of proof.

If my sacrifice, my presentation of myself, is living, alert, ready and fully prepared, then the will of God will always be good to me. The mercy of God that gave me life will lead me always to expect nothing but good from such a Heavenly

Father. Because I now live, He can be nothing but goodness to me.

If the presentation of myself to God is holy, then whatever His will may be, it will be acceptable to me. The word "holy" here means separate, set apart for God, and the word "acceptable" means well-pleasing. Thus if I am truly set apart for God and His purposes, whatever His will may be, it will be well-pleasing to me.

If my offering is acceptable, then I will find His will to be perfect. "Acceptable" again means well-pleasing, and "perfect" here means complete, with nothing missing. How appropriate this third part is then. If I am well-pleasing to God, His will will be complete, nothing will be missing. Thus, if I present myself, I will most surely prove His will to be good, well-pleasing and complete. And so it will come to pass that my prepared heart, ready always to do His will, will never limit the purposes and counsels of God.

Another truth we find in Romans 12:1,2, is that "presentation leads to transformation." As I present my body, living, holy, acceptable to God, the command then comes in verse 2, "Be not conformed to this world: but be ye transformed." This transformation is not something I can do myself. I can only be transformed by the renewing of my mind — or as the Amplified Version says, "by the [entire] renewal of your mind — by its new ideals and its new attitude."

This is the cost of having a prepared heart.

The two verses we looked at from Psalm 78 at the beginning of this chapter, showed us that the children of Israel limited God because their hearts were not prepared, and because they were not steadfast or faithful to God. These two things are necessary for God's service — a prepared heart and a faithful spirit. We have seen the story of the prepared heart in Romans 12:1,2. There is still the need for a faithful, steadfast spirit.

This is wonderfully illustrated in the books of Ezra and Haggai. Ezra follows II Chronicles which ends with the utter destruction of Jerusalem by Nebuchadnezzar, and the city lying in waste for seventy years. II Chronicles 36:22 records how Cyrus King of Persia was moved by God to start the rebuilding of the house of God. This movement by God is also recorded in Ezra. It shows us the challenge coming to the Jews who were living in peace in the land of their captivity, where they had found prosperity. But there were those who, in the words of Romans 12:1, "presented their bodies a living sacrifice." With hearts truly prepared, they left all the comforts they had gathered, and tramped for months to the ruined city of Jerusalem. Here they found nothing but desolation and destruction, and weed-covered ruins. As they struggled on with their building, they encountered difficulties and opposition on every side. Their prepared hearts were being tested to the full.

The book of Haggai also covers the same period. The whole of Haggai consists of thirty-eight verses in two small chapters, but it contains a message especially for the Church today. It was written because somebody said one short sentence. This may sound strange, but it is perfectly true. The reason for the writing of Haggai is seen in chapter 1, verse 2: "This people say, The time is not come, the time that the Lord's house should be built." It is the story of "The Lost Vision," of people who once had a prepared heart, but who failed to have a faithful, steadfast spirit.

These former captives had left all for God, they had suffered much, they were heroes of the faith — but they limited God. Haggai's challenging word is "Consider your ways." The only reason they had ever left their pleasant homes in the Empire of Persia, was to come with a prepared heart to build for God. So Haggai cries (verse 4), "Is it time for you, O ye, to dwell in your cieled houses, and this house lie waste?"

In verse 6 God shows them the results of the lost vision:

> Ye have sown much, and bring in little; ye eat, but ye have not enough; ye drink, but ye are not filled with drink; ye clothe you, but there is none warm; and he that earneth wages earneth wages to put it into a bag with holes.

The result of a lost vision is a life full of dissatisfaction — plenty of effort with little to show for it. Here surely is the message for us today, a challenge to those who set out with a prepared heart, but who fail to remain true and steadfast to the original call. In so doing they limit God, in spite of a separated life.

It is interesting to see in the first chapter of Haggai the whole story of how God deals with those who have lost their vision. First there is the *reason* — they have said "the time is not yet come." Then came the *result* of the lost vision — much activity but little productivity. In verses 7 and 8 we find the *recall* and *reminder* from God:

> Thus saith the Lord of hosts; Consider your ways. Go up to the mountain, and bring wood, and build the house; and I will take pleasure in it, and I will be glorified, saith the Lord.

The ultimate aim of all their work was that God should be glorified. As the old catechism says, "Man's chief aim is to glorify God and to enjoy Him for ever."

Then comes the *repentance* of the people. In verse 12 we read that the rulers "with all the remnant of the people, obeyed the voice of the Lord their God." Finally comes the *return* of God to the midst of His people: "I am with you, saith the Lord."

It is this message of Haggai which is so needed in our churches today. Apart from those who have never had a vision, and who have never presented their whole lives to God, there are many to whom God has spoken in bygone days.

Very often I counsel people who say with a weary heart, "You know, once the things of God meant everything to me. I had committed all to Him and I was so busy and happy serving my Lord." Then they go on to tell how the vision faded, and their burning hearts grew cold. They got taken up with so many other "things" — not necessarily evil or wicked things, but things which absorbed their time, their money and their lives. Eventually they found themselves saying "Yes, of course, the things of God are very important. Yes, I fully intend some day to put in an all-out effort — but not just now. I've got so many other things all lined up, I can't really spare the time." And so the vision fades as they lose their order of priorities. They plunge into a busy world of "things" — good things, honest things maybe, but still just things. They had a prepared heart as had the builders in Haggai's day, but they didn't have a faithful and steadfast spirit.

I saw the opposite of this wonderfully illustrated in a church I visited last year. I was speaking at a midweek prayer meeting in the month of August, and I went to the church expecting to find the faithful few. By the time we began there were nearly three hundred members there, and they all meant business! There is a fine story behind this. The present pastor has been there for about fifteen years. When he came the membership was very small and the impact of the church on the world need was practically nil. But the pastor is, above all else, a man of vision with a wonderfully prepared heart, and a very faithful, steadfast spirit. The church has grown steadily in numbers and vigorously in outlook, with a vision that extends far and wide.

Some time ago it was obvious that the present auditorium was very soon going to be too small for the increasing attendance. So schemes were discussed and plans were made and drawn for a new auditorium. The architect's drawings were hanging in the entrance hall when I went. I was much impressed. The money to rebuild was forthcoming, and before long the building fund was an impressive sight.

Then it was that the prepared heart and the steadfast spirit took over the whole situation. The vision of the church by now was an uplifted vision, their missionary program was live, growing and vigorous. When they viewed the needs of the mission field and then considered their own building fund, they made a tremendous decision. They decided not to spend their money on a vast rebuilding program. Instead they installed closed circuit television in the large hall below, thus doubling their seating capacity. The large sum of money on hand was invested in the larger vision of the greater need elsewhere.

When I heard this story my heart rejoiced. Here was no limitation of God, but the reverse. From this one church there radiates power and life and joy and blessing. Who can measure the untold honor and glory that has been added to the Lamb of God through the witness of this one church? It began almost as a modern counterpart of the book of Ezra. Men and women with prepared hearts came to rebuild a place of failure. They found destruction, opposition and persecution, but there was also a continuing, faithful, steadfast spirit which had a glorious vision. This vision remains, enhanced, uplifted, outreaching, and God is at work, unlimited in His blessing.

Many churches, as bodies of believers, possess this same vision. They have recognized why they are called out, and they have maintained the vision steadfastly and faithfully. As a church they have "a prepared heart" and a "presented body" which is truly living, holy and acceptable.

There is one other side of this truth which needs to be considered in connection with the story of Ezra and Haggai. Not only were the people called out as a body to rebuild the temple, but each one had his own individual responsibility to God.

So we personally have our own responsibility to God today. When we consider I Corinthians 6:19,20, we can find a message for our own hearts today.

> What? know ye not that your body is the temple of the Holy Ghost which is in you, which ye have of God, and ye are not your own? For ye are bought with a price: therefore glorify God in your body, and in your spirit, which are God's . . .

The ultimate purpose of the coming of Christ was to restore our true humanity. As He said in John 10:10, "I am come that they might have life, and that they might have it more abundantly." God's salvation is not merely the forgiveness of sins, but the restoration of life in the person of the Holy Spirit of Christ.

Psalm 69 is one of those precious psalms that speaks of the crucifixion of Christ, as verse 21 especially tells us: "They gave me also gall for my meat; and in my thirst they gave me vinegar to drink." The last phrase of verse 4 contains a jewel of truth: ". . . *then I restored that which I took not away.*" Applying this to Christ's death, as He was dealing with the whole question of our salvation, He not only bore our sins in His own body on the tree, but He also dealt with the problems of the restoration of life.

This aspect of the work of Christ is sometimes overlooked, or almost ignored, in considering the great work of salvation. So often the emphasis is placed on the forgiveness of sins, as if that was the most important part of the work of Christ. John gives us the last word, as it were, on the purpose of the Gospel, in chapter 20, verses 30 and 31:

> And many other signs truly did Jesus in the presence of his disciples, which are not written in this book: but these are written, that ye might believe that Jesus is the Christ, the Son of God; and that believing ye might have life through his name.

The ultimate aim of the Gospel — "that ye might have life through his name."

The phrase *"through his name"* is a literal rendering of the original, but has little meaning for us in English. We read it only as words with no real inner significance — "through his name" — nor do the words make us stop and think. But in the Amplified Version the phrase (both here and in other places) becomes alive — "through His name [that is, through what He is]." Now the whole phrase is charged with power — "that ye might have life through what He is."

When we put this truth with verse 4 of Psalm 69, the inner meaning is revealed. *"Then I restored that which I took not away."* Jesus Christ restored life — spiritual life, eternal life — through what He is. In other words, the life He restored wasn't an item, a thing, an "it," but Himself. "I am the way, the truth and the life," He said. He Himself was the life that He restored.

It is lovely to put that verse alongside John 1:29. "The next day John seeth Jesus coming unto him, and saith, Behold the Lamb of God which taketh away the sin of the world." We can now see again the twofold work of Christ. He took away that which He did not commit (our sin). He restored that which He took not away (our life).

That great text, John 3:16, has the same twofold idea: "For God so loved the world, that he gave his only begotten Son, that whosoever believeth in him should not perish [dealing with the sin question], but have everlasting life [dealing with the restoration of life]." I John 5:11,12 is dogmatic on this point —

> And this is the record, that God hath given to us eternal life, and this life is in his Son. He that hath the Son hath life; and he that hath not the Son of God hath not life.

John 3:16 shows both the negative side of my salvation (my sin dealt with) and the positive side (the restoration of life). So much weak and feeble Christian living comes from a negative appreciation of the work of Christ. The negative side was necessary, vitally necessary, but not as an end in itself. It was necessary that my sin should be dealt with, but only as a means of bringing me into a right relationship with God, in order that I might have life by virtue of who and what He is.

Therefore when I read I Corinthians 6:19,20, and see that my body is the temple of the Holy Ghost, I realize that the One who indwells me is the Lord Jesus in the person of His Holy Spirit. Romans 8:9 is quite definite on this point: "Now if any man have not the Spirit of Christ, he is none of his." Jesus Christ indwells by His Holy Spirit. The life has been restored, but has the temple been rebuilt? Our verse in Haggai 1:2 described those who said, "The time is not come, the time that the Lord's house should be built." You remember, the only reason they ever left their place of pleasurable captivity to go to a ruined and desolate area was to rebuild the Temple of God, for Him to find pleasure and be glorified in it.

So it is with us. The ultimate purpose of our salvation is not that we should escape a coming judgment, but that we might live for His pleasure and to His glory. This is attained when the "temple is rebuilt." I Kings 8:60,61, records part of King Solomon's blessing of the people when the first earthly Temple was dedicated —

> That all the people of the earth may know that the Lord is God, and that there is none else. Let your heart therefore be perfect with the Lord our God. . . .

God replied to Solomon's consecration:

> I have heard thy prayer and thy supplication, that thou hast made before me: I have hallowed this house, which thou hast built, to put my name there for ever; and mine eyes and mine heart shall be there perpetually (I Kings 9:3).

When the Temple was properly completed and faithfully dedicated, God promised that His name, His eyes and His heart would be there for ever.

But to us God has given a more precious promise — not only His name, His eyes and His heart, but Himself, God the Son, in the power of His Holy Spirit. The trinity of prom-

ise for Solomon becomes the trinity of persons for us. What
was "his name" for Solomon's day, is for us "God the Father."
What was "his eyes" is for us "God the Holy Spirit." What was
for Solomon "his heart" is for us "God the Son." May we
realize the honor and the dignity which is ours in being the
temple of God. With the men of Haggai's day may we see
and admit the failure and weakness in our lives.

> Ye have sown much, and bring in little; ye eat, but ye have not
> enough; ye drink, but ye are not filled with drink; ye clothe you,
> but there is none warm; and he that earneth wages earneth wages
> to put it into a bag with holes. . . . Ye looked for much, and, lo,
> it came to little; . . . Why? saith the Lord of hosts. Because of
> mine house that is waste. . . .

A humble act of self-examination will show us that unless we
rebuild a Temple that is holy and pure and for His glory, we
can never know fruit that remains, feeding that really satisfies, fellowship that abides, and service that brings glory to
God, grace to others, and eventually gladness to our own
hearts.

If God is to be unlimited in our lives then it will only
be as He is unlimited in our daily living. Our body physically,
mentally and morally must be prepared as a temple of God.
Holiness must not be only a word in a book, it must be interpreted into the fiber of our daily life. A holy temple is a
Spirit-filled temple, which means an exalted Christ, and an
unlimited God.

CHAPTER 5

LIMITING GOD THROUGH UNBELIEF

IF WE WILL READ PSALM 78 again, we will find another characteristic of the children of Israel which can be a warning to us. It is found in two verses:

> They believed not in God, and trusted not in his salvation (verse 22). For all this they sinned still, and believed not for his wondrous works (verse 32).

This must surely seem very strange to us. The children of Israel had seen the hand of God at work in Egypt, they had been most wonderfully redeemed, their needs had been met and their wants supplied. Yet they did not believe God. It sounds fantastic that this should be so, but it was. In spite of all that God had done for them, they still questioned His ability and His purpose. "Can God furnish a table in the wilderness?" they asked (verse 19). So they limited God through unbelief. They had enough belief to get themselves out of Egypt, but not enough to get themselves into Canaan. The promises of God were made, the assurance from God was given, the wealth of Canaan was theirs the moment they left Egypt, but because of unbelief they did not enter in and God was limited through their unbelief.

Unbelief is characteristic of many of God's people, both in the Bible and in the church today. Jacob's life exemplifies the results of unbelief in the promises of God. In Genesis 27 we

have recorded the story of the stolen blessing. Isaac, feeling
his end near, sent his favorite son Esau to the field to hunt
for deer. Esau was to prepare venison for his father so that
his father could eat and bless him. Rebekah heard all this,
and she instructed Jacob, Esau's twin, her favorite, so that
he could acquire the blessing. The story is one long record
of lies, deceit and trickery. Jacob blatantly said he found the
deer "because the Lord thy God brought it to me" — what
blasphemy! The story ends with the reader feeling very sorry
for the villain, Esau, and utterly repulsed with the behavior
of Jacob, the hero — because Jacob *was* God's man. It is in
this story that Jacob lives up to the meaning of his name —
deceiver, liar, twister.

The whole point of this miserable story is that it need
never have happened, it was so unnecessary. It all came because of Jacob's unbelief. God had already made His promise
(Genesis 25:23). He had already said that the elder would
serve the younger. He had already promised both the birthright and the blessing to Jacob. Rebekah knew all this because
the promise was made to her at her request — She had in-
quired of the Lord (Genesis 25:22). Thus she knew the promises from the very beginning. Jacob was her favorite son, and
no mother ever keeps back anything from her favorite son.
Esau was the strong man, the man who could get things done,
while Jacob was the weakling, the one who liked to be about
the house, the domestic type. But Rebekah must surely have
comforted him with the knowledge that all was to be his, that
he was to succeed his father Isaac.

Although Jacob knew the promises of God, he prepared
his own plans to get what God had already promised — the
perfect example of unbelief. He need never have lifted a
finger, and both the birthright and the blessing would have
come to him — God had promised it so. In God's own time,
and in God's own way, all the promises for Jacob would have

come true. But Jacob couldn't wait, he couldn't keep his hands off the promises of God. He planned and lied and schemed and deceived to get what was already his.

God had made promises, Jacob had made his own plans, so Jacob had to pay the price of unbelief. Galatians 6:7 is true for all time and for all types: "Be not deceived; God is not mocked: for whatsoever a man soweth, that shall he also reap." This verse contains a warning, a truth and a law. The warning — "be not deceived." The truth — "God is not mocked." The law — "whatsoever a man soweth, that shall he also reap."

Jacob was deceived. He who was the arch deceiver was deceived by his own heart. Jacob mocked God. His very planning was a proof of his disbelief, and disbelief is the height of mockery. Jacob was to reap a harvest through all his life because of his unbelief. As a result of his trickery, Esau swore to kill him. Rebekah in her anxiety for her beloved son said to him, "Arise, flee thou to Laban my brother to Haran; and tarry with him a few days, until thy brother's fury turn away" (Genesis 27:43,44). To save his life, Jacob left the home he loved and the mother he loved, for "*just a few days.*" But listen to his voice crying out in distress in chapter 31:38: "This twenty years have I been with thee." The few days turned into over twenty years. Over twenty years of separation from the home he loved and from the mother he adored. The price that Jacob paid for his unbelief was to lose the very thing he loved most — his home life.

Even when his own family came, and he had a home of his own, it was never a happy home full of love and tenderness. His own children grew up to lie to him, to cheat him and to deceive him. Jacob certainly reaped a hundredfold the seeds of deceit that he sowed that day. And his experiences during those twenty years with Laban were utterly humiliating. He was tricked and deceived by both his uncle and his cousins. With no one to turn to he must have felt the bitterness that he himself had put in the heart of Esau.

But the point was, it was so unnecessary. If only Jacob had believed God, and rested on the promises of God, all the goodness would have been his without the ·grief. But no — God promised, Jacob planned, and then he paid the bitter price of unbelief. Just as the children of Israel limited God by their unbelief, so the plans of Jacob limited the fullness of joy that might have been his.

Another great character in whose life we can learn the same lesson is Abraham. In Genesis 13 we read that after Lot had made his choice to go to the well-watered plain of Jordan, God made a promise to Abram. (His name had not yet been changed to Abraham.)

> And the Lord said unto Abram, after that Lot was separated from him, Lift up now thine eyes, and look . . . for all the land which thou seest, to thee will I give it, and to thy seed for ever (Genesis 13:14,15).

There was the beginning of the promise — a son for Abraham. Sometime later the whole matter was raised again. Abraham asked God (in chapter 15:2), "Lord God, what wilt thou give me, seeing I go childless. . . ." God promised him, in verse 4, a son out of his own body and a succession of seed as many as the stars of heaven. Verse 6 distinctly says that Abraham "believed in the Lord; and he counted it to him for righteousness." Paul makes much of the faith of Abraham in Romans 4, even quoting Genesis 15:6: "For what saith the scripture? Abraham believed God, and it was counted unto him for righteousness" (verse 4).

Abraham is indeed the father of the faithful, but he wasn't always so. There was a time when, like his grandson Jacob, he heard the promises of God and believed them, but then went on to make his own plans. Genesis 16 contains this story of the unbelief of the believer.

After God had renewed his promise in Genesis 15, Abraham waited for the son to come. He waited one year, two years, three, four . . . ten years — but no son came. So it was that he took a hand in the matter and planned to get what God had already promised. He had only to await God's time, but that proved to be too long. Chapter 16 begins,

> Now Sarai, Abram's wife bare him no children: and she had an handmaid, an Egyptian, whose name was Hagar. And Sarai said unto Abram, Behold now, the Lord hath restrained me from bearing: I pray thee, go in unto my maid; it may be that I may obtain children by her. And Abram hearkened to the voice of Sarai. And Sarai Abram's wife took Hagar her maid the Egyptian, after Abram had dwelt ten years in the land of Canaan, and gave her to her husband Abram to be his wife.

So Abraham married Hagar and immediately Hagar conceived and a child was born — a son! Abraham had planned and gotten what God had already promised. But just as in Jacob's case where God had promised and Abraham planned, then a price had to be paid. Abraham sowed but he had also to reap.

The first thing was a breakdown of family relationships. Sarah was despised by her maid, and in her bitter reaction Abraham was left with two wives in opposition to each other. Domestic happiness was gone. Then God gave His verdict on Abraham's plan. He said of the son to be born, "He will be a wild man; his hand will be against every man, and every man's hand against him" (16:12). Imagine peaceful Abraham having a son who would be a wild man. But then Ishmael wasn't the son of God's promise but of Abraham's plan.

Genesis 21 tells us of the fulfillment of God's promise:

> And the Lord visited Sarah as he had said, and the Lord did unto Sarah as he had spoken. For Sarah conceived, and bare Abraham a son in his old age, at the set time of which God had spoken to him.

Ishmael was fourteen years old when Isaac was born! Abraham had to wait not ten years but twenty-four years! But it all came true as God had promised.

This isn't the end of the story, however, because there was still Ishmael, the wild man whose hand was to be raised against every man and every man's hand against him. He wasn't God's promise, but see how Abraham loved him: "And Abraham said unto God, O that Ishmael might live before thee!" (17:18). Abraham wanted God to support his plan, so that Ishmael might become the child of promise. He had schemed to produce a son, but Ishmael wasn't the son who would inherit. In fact a simple Bible study will show us what happened to the descendants of Ishmael.

In Genesis 37 we have the story of Joseph, God's man. In this story he is taken captive to Egypt. Who was it who took him down to Egypt? The Ishmaelites! The descendants of "Abraham's plan" took a son of "God's promise" down to Egypt as a captive. How amazing! Little did Abraham realize what his plan would lead to.

If we look at Psalm 83 we come to a series of verses that are both fact and prophecy. The psalm begins with a call for help. The enemies of Israel are scheming and combining against God's people.

> They have said, Come, and let us cut them off from being a nation: that the name of Israel may be no more in remembrance. For they have consulted together with one consent: they are confederate against thee: The tabernacles of Edom and the Ishmaelites (verses 4-6).

In the days of the psalmist the Ishmaelites were scheming and combining with others to wipe out Israel. Now the descendants of "Abraham's plan" were fighting against the whole people of Israel — open persecution.

But the most amazing thing about this psalm is its prophecy which is being fulfilled even in our day. Today there is a Kingdom of Israel once more. Israel has a set of enemies that have consulted together and made a confederation against her — the United Arab Republic under President Nasser. President Nasser's aim is to "cut them off from being a nation: that the name of Israel may be no more in remembrance." This is his avowed policy. Even today, he is surrounding Israel with airfields from which an all-out attack may be made. Who is this President Nasser? He is a descendant of Ishmael, whose mother was an Egyptian!

So we have the fantastic fact that, humanly speaking, Abraham's plan is at the root of all the trouble in the Middle East. Ishmael is still at war with Isaac. What a price has been paid throughout all the years of struggle between Abraham's plan and God's promise. First it was against the man Joseph. Then it was against the people of Israel. Now it is against the whole nation. There is trouble now, not with a man, nor a people, but with the whole of the Middle East.

God made a promise to Abraham, to Jacob, and to the Jews in Egypt. In each case the promise was accepted but it was never properly received. There was always that undercurrent of unbelief — the unbelief of the believer. In all this God was limited — through unbelief.

I Corinthians 10 tells us that as we read these stories we will find types of our own behavior. So let us take warning. For, if God so dealt with His people the Jews, if they had a price to pay and a harvest to reap, how much more will this be true of us. Has God made any promises to us that might compare in magnitude with those to His people of old? If we look at II Peter 1:4 we find that God has "given unto us exceeding great and precious promises." Notice the unique choice of language. These are not just *promises*, not merely *precious promises*, not only *great and precious promises*, but *exceeding great and precious promises*.

The Word of God uses a trinity of superlatives to describe

the amazing quality of promises given to us. Such promises must be unique, and so they are. Verse 4 goes on to say, "that by these ye might be partakers of the divine nature." I must confess that when I first saw these words and considered them I felt as if the thought was somewhat blasphemous. That I should be made a partaker of God's nature sounds utterly preposterous. I have one nature already, a fallen human nature which is ever prone to sin. But now the Word of God teaches that I can be a partaker of another nature, the divine nature.

When I consider this against the background of other Scriptures, however, I can understand more fully what is being taught. I John 5:11, 12 tells me plainly, "that God hath given to us eternal life, and this life is in his Son. He that hath the Son hath life; and he that hath not the Son of God hath not life." I John 4:4 says, "Ye are of God . . . because greater is he that is in you, than he that is in the world." The Amplified Version has a delightful translation of I John 3:24.

> All who keep His commandments (who obey His orders and follow His plan, live and continue to live, to stay and) abide in Him, and He in them. . . . They let Christ be a home to them and they are the home of Christ. And by this we know *and* understand *and* have the proof that He [really] lives *and* makes His home in us, by the (Holy) Spirit Whom He has given us.

So that I really am a partaker of the divine nature. Jesus Christ lives in me in the person of His Holy Spirit. I have life, and life isn't an "it" but a Person. Jesus told Thomas, "I am the way, the truth, and the life: no man cometh unto the Father but by me" (John 14:6). Jesus is the Life and He lives in me — this is the exceeding great and precious promise.

What does this promise offer me? To Abraham the promise was a son; to Jacob the promise was the birthright and the blessing; to the Jews from Egypt the promise was Canaan. The promises were given, but they were not taken up as they should have been, and we have seen that the result was a harvest of sorrow for the individual, and a deliberate limita-

tion of God. Could you be guilty of planning to get by your
own efforts that which is yours by divine promise? The Amplified Version of I John 5:18 may be able to help us on this
point:

> We know [absolutely] that anyone born of God does not [de-
> liberately and knowingly] practice committing sin, but the One
> Who was begotten of God carefully watches over *and* protects
> him — Christ's divine presence within him preserves him against
> the evil — and the wicked one does not lay hold (get a grip) on
> him *or* touch [him].

This verse points to a high and holy quality of living, the
very thing the Christian Church needs today. It suggests that
there is a life to be lived which is sparkling in its purity, the
kind of life that unconsciously challenges the normal drab
grays of other lives. This life can be mine right now, the
promise says. I am a partaker of the divine nature, and
Christ's divine presence within me preserves me against the
evil.

All this we believe in a hazy, theoretical way — just as
Abraham and Jacob believed. But like them, we start to make
plans of our own. We determine that our lives shall be improved and we work out our own plans for doing so. We turn
over new leaves, we pray more, read more, try new gimmicks
on holiness. In short, we do all we can to make our fallen
human nature acceptable to God. Paul, however, could say
in Romans 7:18, "For I know that in me (that is, in my
flesh) dwelleth no good thing." But we don't go as far as that.
We like to say, "Well, I know I'm not perfect, I do many
things I shouldn't do, but, after all, there are some good points
about me." Paul could say *no good thing* about himself apart
from God. He told the Ephesians that before they were Christians they were *dead in trespasses and sins* (2:1), and he included himself in that description (2:5). That is why he
could say in Galatians 2:20,

> I am crucified with Christ: nevertheless I live; yet not I, but Christ liveth in me: and the life which I now live in the flesh I live by the faith of the Son of God, who loved me and gave himself for me.

Spiritually Paul was dead and corrupt — the only life in him was the life of Christ. So many Christians slip up on this point. They think that Christ came to change our deadness into a quality of life so that we can now struggle on with this patched-up human nature — as though our fallen human nature had been magically restored to life so that now we can do what we couldn't do before. It is at this point that we plan and scheme to get what God has promised. We know that God has promised joy and peace through victory over sin, and this we try to achieve with our patched-up human nature.

The epistle to the Colossians was written to true Christians. Yet in chapter 3, Paul tells them,

> For ye are dead, and your life is hid with Christ in God. When Christ, who is our life, shall appear, then shall ye also appear with him in glory (verses 3,4).

Paul told the Ephesians they *were* dead before they became true Christians (2:1). He told the Colossians, "Ye *are* dead" — you are still dead, your human nature is still corrupt, sinful and no good (3:3,4). The only life in you is Christ. In John 14:6 Jesus said that He was the life. He also said, "Because I live, ye shall live also" (John 14:19). The only possibility of my living is when Jesus comes to live His life in me. God's promise was not a patch-up but a Person.

This is where we fall into the error of Abraham, and Jacob. We recognize the need for a higher quality of living, and in spite of God's promise, we seek to produce by our own efforts that quality of life that God has promised. The price we pay is frustration, bitter disappointment, decreasing effort and a lowering of our standards. For if we cannot reach the standards we have set, then we must lower our standards of living until we can meet them. No, we must accept this *exceeding great and precious promise.* In humbleness and true confession we must admit our utter ruin, deadness and loss. Then we must embrace the glorious truth that, although I am written off as a failure, there now lives in me One who is my life. I can come to a place where the truth of Philippians 4:13 begins to dawn in my heart, "I can do all things through Christ which strengtheneth me." The Amplified Version brings out the full meaning,

> I have strength for all things in Christ Who empowers me — I am ready for anything and equal to anything through Him Who infuses inner strength into me, [that is, I am self-sufficient in Christ's sufficiency].

The great challenge is whether we will admit the utter worthlessness of our fallen human nature and own up to our total spiritual deadness and bankruptcy. It will be helpful to recall that the Word of God records three cases where Christ raised the dead to life. One was Lazarus, whose deadness was utter corruption and with whom there was nothing pleasant or lovely. Another was the son of the widow of Nain. His body was cold and dead, though no corruption was as yet evident. The third was the daughter of Jairus. She had just died, her body was warm, and there was a loveliness about her form and features — but she was still dead. Each of the three had a different outward appearance — utter corruption, cold stiffness, warm loveliness — but they were all dead. All three needed one thing, physical life.

Physical death is not always horrible and repulsive at first, but it soon leads to complete and utter corruption. There is only one answer to death, and that is life. No material benefits or rewards, no earthly honors or glories can meet the need — only life. The same is true of spiritual death. This was why Christ said to religious people, "I am come that they might have life, and that they might have it more abundantly" (John 10:10). The people to whom He spoke had the purest religion in the world, the finest laws ever written, the richest teaching from the lips of the blessed Lord Himself — but they were still spiritually dead. He came that they might have life. Notice He didn't say that they might live, but that they might have *life*. In other words, into their hearts, alongside their spiritually dead human nature, would come *life* in the person of His Holy Spirit.

So it is in your life and mine. When we become true Christians we are born again, we receive life. This life is the presence of Christ in the person of His Holy Spirit. It is in this way that I become a partaker of the divine nature. But the essential point is that when He comes to be my life, He is the only Life I have, He is my only source of power, joy, peace and victory. All *I* can do is fail, as I have proved all through my life. All *He* can do is succeed, as He has proved all through His life.

With this truth firmly in our hearts let us look once more at some of the verses quoted above. I John 5:18 (Amplified Version):

> We know [absolutely] that anyone born of God does not [deliberately and knowingly] practice committing sin, but the One Who was begotten of God carefully watches over *and* protects him — Christ's divine presence within preserves him against the evil — and the wicked one does not lay hold (get a grip) on him *or* touch [him].

I can know a peace and a joy through victory over sin, but I am not gaining the victory. The victory comes as I recognize, first my utter helplessness to succeed, and second that Christ's divine peace within me preserves me. There is victory — but it must be His victory.

We read in I Corinthians 15:57, "But thanks be to God, which giveth us the victory through our Lord Jesus Christ." Our victory is the gift of God, worked out through our Lord Jesus Christ. Let me repeat it: this victory is the gift of God; it can only be ours when we take it! Victory isn't something I win, but something I receive as a gift from God. Just as in

the days when we heard the Gospel as sinners, our forgiveness was not by works of righteousness which we had done,
but it was the gift of God. Many of us were too proud at first
to come and admit our need, and then to receive from the
hands of God a full and a free pardon for all our sin, but
eventually we did — otherwise we would still be in our sins.
So it is with living the Christian life. The deadness that separated me from God still remains, but Christ is my life, and
I can know victory and daily blessing as I relate everything
to Him.

Philippians 4:13 (Amplified Version) says:

> I have strength for all things in Christ Who empowers me — I am
> ready for anything and equal to anything through Him Who in-
> fuses inner strength into me, [that is, I am self-sufficient in Christ's
> sufficiency].

We saw in I John 5:18 that the presence of Christ is the
answer to my sin and temptation — "Christ's divine presence
within preserves . . . against the evil." Now we can see that
the presence of Christ is the answer to all my service. *Strength
for all things — ready for anything — equal to anything.* How
wide the horizons become when we relate our service to
Christ. We are completely self-sufficient in Christ's sufficiency. I can have all that He is for all that I need. Truly we
can say with the psalmist in Psalm 121:

> I will lift up mine eyes unto the hills, from whence cometh my
> help. My help cometh from the Lord, which made heaven and
> earth.

How often have we believed that our help comes from the
Lord? We have believed instead that if we did our best, and
worked hard then God would come and add His share to
that which we had done. In other words, like Abraham and
Jacob, we believed the promises of God but made our own
plans.

How often we have reaped a harvest of bitter disappointment and felt the fury of frustration — we have done so much

and it all came to nothing. Here is God's answer for us — *have strength for all things in Christ — and in Christ alone!* Everything I do bears the mark of death and corruption because "that which is . . . of the flesh is flesh"! But when I relate everything to Him, when I spread it out before Him and commit it to Him, then it becomes His responsibility.

Let me finish this chapter with a prayer. Perhaps God has spoken to you and you want to claim "all that He is for all that you need."

A Prayer of Realization

Heavenly Father,

Forgive my blindness and stupidity. For so long I have tried to fight for You and live for You in my own strength. How disappointing it has been, how fruitless, how I have limited You. O God, You have promised, but I have planned — and failed.

Now, Father, I confess my failure. I confess that I have planned to get what You have already promised. I confess that I have a nature which is corrupt and dead. It always has been so, it always will be so. But I now believe that I am a partaker of Your divine nature, that Jesus Christ lives in me through the Holy Spirit. I now believe that He is my Life, the only Life I can ever have or need. Nothing less could satisfy, nothing more is possible.

I believe and recognize that He is my victory over sin and temptation. Grant that He may move into every sphere of my life. Grant to me an obedient heart to crown Him Lord of all.

I thank You also that He, Jesus alone, is my strength for all service. "I have strength for all things in Christ Who empowers me." Help me to live in the good of this, and to relate and expose every experience and situation to Him who indwells me by His Holy Spirit.

Heavenly Father, I offer myself now as a vehicle for the life of Christ. I am available. "Here am I, send me!"

For Christ's sake. Amen.

CHAPTER 6

LIMITING GOD THROUGH DISOBEDIENCE

WE HAVE BEEN CONSIDERING, so far, the ways in which God's own people limited God. In I Corinthians 10:1-4 there are some unusual things said about the children of Israel. Notice the fivefold use of the word *all*.

> ... all our fathers were under the cloud, and all passed through the sea; and were all baptized unto Moses in the cloud and in the sea; and did all eat the same spiritual meat; and did all drink the same spiritual drink: for they drank of that spiritual Rock that followed them: and that Rock was Christ.

From the reading of these verses, with the emphasis on the word *all*, we have a picture of a 100 per cent church — a called-out people with an outward united spiritual experience. Any pastor today would be glad if such unity was expressed among his own people, especially if there was the eating of the same spiritual meat and the drinking of that Rock which is Christ. Yet when we come to verse 5 in our passage we meet a big *but*: "But with many of them God was not well pleased." In spite of all the outward unity and correctness of spiritual experience the whole situation was shattered by failure. God was not well pleased and they were overthrown in the wilderness. This can be true in our present-day churches. We can have that outward appearance of agreement, that unity of purpose, that dependence on Christ for meat and drink and still be displeasing to God. The wilder-

77

ness is the place where people wander and murmur and are overthrown, in spite of outward unity.

In Psalm 78:8 another cause for limiting God is seen: "And might not be as their fathers, a stubborn and rebellious generation." Verse 10 adds that "they kept not the covenant of God, and refused to walk in his law." Behind all their outward appearances, there was a continuous current of disobedience. In Egypt they had been compelled to obey by the whip and cruelty of the taskmasters. But now, having been delivered from their slavery, they indulged in open disobedience in every area of behavior.

We can follow these people and their descendants one stage further if we turn to Joshua 23. Here we are at the close of Joshua's life. After the death of Moses, Joshua had been called to lead the people into the land of Canaan and had done his work successfully. Now he is 110 years old (Joshua 24:29). He had a range of experience which began in Egypt as a slave, and continued on through all the thrill of deliverance by the "passover lamb." With Caleb, he had joined the other ten spies at Kadesh and had made the survey of the promised land (Numbers 13:16). He had lived through all the forty years of empty wandering. He had been chosen by God to lead the people in, and to lead them on in conquest of the land that was theirs. All this he had faithfully accomplished, and now his life is drawing to a close.

In chapters 23 and 24, Joshua is moved to bring one last challenge to these people with whom he has lived and suffered and endured for over three generations. He knows their disobedient hearts, and how rebellious they have been, resisting every inch of the way. Now he makes his last stand for God, seeking once more to turn these people to the Lord their God.

To do this Joshua "called for all Israel, and for their elders, and for their heads, and for their judges, and for their

officers" (23:2). See how this verse links up with our open-
ing thoughts from I Corinthians 10 on the 100 per cent church
— once more *all* the people are being involved. In verse 3
Joshua gives God all the glory: "Ye have seen all that the
Lord your God hath done unto all these nations because of
you; for the Lord your God is he that hath fought for you."
He goes on to speak of their inheritance and adds, in verse 5,
these remarkable words: "The Lord your God, he shall expel
them . . . and ye shall possess their land." Here was the promise of future success and of how it would be accomplished. In
verse 6 he re-echoes the words God spoke to him in Joshua
1:7: "Be ye therefore very courageous to keep and to do all
that is written in the book of the law of Moses."

Finally in chapter 24 Joshua gets down to business. He
realizes it is no good just to talk to the people and to challenge
them with encouraging words. He moves in with all the
authority of God: "Thus saith the Lord God of Israel." Then
God speaks through his aged servant. Notice how He reminds
the people of all that He had done: *I took . . . I led . . . I gave
. . . I sent . . . I plagued . . . I brought you out . . . I gave them
. . . I destroyed them.* Then in verse 13 God brings the account
right up to date: "I have given you a land for which ye did
not labour, and cities which ye built not, and ye dwell in
them."

Then comes the crashing challenge of verse 14: "Now
therefore fear the Lord, and serve him in sincerity and in
truth." Joshua is moved by the outpoured gladness and mercy
and forgiveness of God. In all the dignity of age and the
wealth of experience he takes his last fighting stand for God:
"Choose you this day whom ye will serve . . . but as for me
and my house, we will serve the Lord."

As we look at the way in which Joshua deals with a
people noted for their constant failure and disobedience, let
us remember the instruction of I Corinthians 10. These words

of Joshua and his handling of the situation are applicable to us today. The same Holy Spirit who inspired the writing of these passages can also speak to our hearts as we read these words. This book is not written to interest people, or to educate people, but to be used by the Holy Spirit to change hearts and lives — maybe your heart and life.

See then how Joshua begins by calling the children of Israel to a *real choice.* They were not to go home and think about it, or discuss the matter, or pass an opinion on the speech — they were to make a definite choice. This is something our human nature tries to avoid. Even in the things of ordinary life it is so much easier to pass the buck, to let someone else make the choice. It is easier to fall in with a choice made by someone else because, if we get tired of the decision, we can always back out on the grounds that it was not our decision. Joshua knew his people and the hardness of their hearts, so he insisted on a real choice.

He also told them to choose "this day" — not this week, this month or this year. He wanted and demanded business to be done there and then. This is the kind of treatment we need. We are in possession of all the facts, we know the unfailing goodness of God, we know our own continual weakness and disobedience. It is good for us, for you and me, to be brought to the point of real decision, of choosing whom we are going to serve. In Matthew 6:24, Jesus challenged the people in his day:

> No man can serve two masters: for either he will hate the one, and love the other; or else he will hold to the one, and despise the other. Ye cannot serve God and mammon.

Our problem is that we think we *can* serve two masters. I am continually meeting Christians in different countries who are busy trying to learn the technique of serving two masters. They do this, and fail miserably, because they have never been brought to the point of making a real choice for God.

It is interesting to study the psychological response of the people of Joshua's challenge to make a real choice. They immediately flung back an answer full of heroism and glowing devotion: "God forbid that we should forsake the Lord, to serve other gods" (verse 16). In verses 17 and 18 they re-echo all the good things that God had done on their behalf and they end with the pious promise: "therefore will we also serve the Lord; for he is our God." One can almost see the horror written on their faces; how could they possibly serve other gods and forsake Jehovah!

But Joshua knew his people, he wasn't taken in by their pious promises and devoted declarations. In verse 19 he unmasked their hypocrisy: "Ye cannot serve the Lord: for he is a holy God." Their words were just lip service, spoken on the spur of the moment with no conviction behind them.

Then Joshua called the people to face up to a *responsible choice*. Choosing to serve God isn't simply a casual committal or a pleasant procedure. It is a realization first that I am dealing with a holy God. These people were quite prepared to switch their allegiance to God through the saying of a few carefully chosen words, but in Joshua's eyes, they had missed the whole point of his challenge. The holiness of God was that which gripped the mind and attention of Joshua. To him God was first and foremost holy, and every approach and arrangement had to be made on this basis. Joshua called the people to reconsider their choice, to recognize that the God to whom they were committing themselves was "a holy God; he is a jealous God."

This is also a great truth for our day and generation. The holiness of God is a lost subject in much of our teaching. In many churches God seems to be merely happy, not holy. As long as we all keep happy and things go well, then — who cares! If we today lose sight of the holiness of God we do so to our own loss, both in purity and in power. We need to be reminded constantly that Calvary was necessary — just because of the holiness of God. In Matthew 27:46 is recorded the agonizing cry of the dying Saviour: "My God, my God, why hast thou forsaken me?" This question was never answered — because the answer had already been given. Jesus was quoting from Psalm 22 in His cry — the crucifixion psalm which gives in amazing detail some of the sufferings of the Saviour. It begins with this agonizing question, and the answer to it is in verse 3. "But thou art holy, O thou that inhabitest the praises of Israel." We, today, in our response to Christian service, need to face up to this great challenge.

After Joshua had called them to consider their choice and to make it truly responsible, the people replied in verse 21: "Nay, but we will serve the Lord." In spite of Joshua's correction they still meant business with God. His reply is in verse 22.

> Ye are witnesses against yourselves that ye have chosen you the Lord, to serve him. And they said, We are witnesses.

Joshua then challenged them to a *repentant choice*. "Now therefore put away . . . the strange gods which are among you, and incline your heart unto the Lord God of Israel" (verse 23). In other words, if they really meant what they said in their desire to serve a holy God, then the first thing to do was to clean up their lives. Notice that Joshua called for a twofold repentance — to put away the strange gods and to turn to the Lord.

This is something we often miss in our modern preaching and teaching. We are apt to call people to believe the Gospel, and what we imply is that they should simply come and accept Jesus as their Saviour, the One who died for them on the cross. This is right as far as it goes, but it does not go far enough. Joshua did not only call the people to turn their hearts to the Lord. He first asked them to put away the strange gods among them. This is the scriptural order of response to God. I do not simply come and believe the Gospel. The scriptural order is *repent and believe.* Before I do business with God I put away the strange gods which are in my heart. This is true for Joshua's time. It is also true in the other books of the Old Testament — and in the New Testament. The Word of God is consistent on this subject.

Repentance was the key word of the preaching of John the Baptist. "Repent ye: for the kingdom of heaven is at hand," was his theme (Matthew 3:2,8,11). This was also part of Christ's first preaching (Mark 1:15): "The time is fulfilled, and the kingdom of God is at hand: repent ye, and believe the gospel." (Notice the order—repent and believe.) Jesus Christ described His purpose in Mark 2:17: "I came not to call the righteous, but sinners to repentance." He sent forth the twelve (Mark 6:12), "and they went out, and preached that men should repent." Listen to the words of Jesus concerning the joy of heaven, given to us twice by Luke: "Likewise, I say unto you, there is joy in the presence of the angels of God over one sinner that repenteth" (15:10,7).

In other words, actions speak louder than words. Believing is a matter of words, but repentance is an act of the will and an attitude of the heart. It isn't the believing that causes the joy in heaven, but the repenting. When Jesus commissioned His disciples, He said to them:

> Thus it is written, and thus it behoved Christ to suffer, and to rise from the dead the third day: and that repentance and remission of sins should be preached in his name among all nations (Luke 24:46,47).

The commission is to preach *repentance and remission of sins* — not merely "Come to Jesus and get your sins forgiven!"

The sermons recorded in Acts show how faithful the early church was in obeying this injunction to preach *repentance and remission.* Peter's great speech on the day of Pentecost ended with these words: "Repent, and be baptized every one of you in the name of Jesus Christ for the remission of sins" (Acts 2:38). Likewise his great speech at the gate Beautiful ends with these words: "Repent ye therefore, and be converted . . ." (Acts 3:19). Paul, speaking at the Areopagus in Athens to the philosophers of his day, concluded his message by saying, "God . . . now commandeth all men everywhere to repent" (Acts 17:30). When he vindicated his divine call before King Agrippa, Paul described it in these words:

> Whereupon, O king Agrippa, I was not disobedient unto the heavenly vision: but shewed first unto them of Damascus, and at Jerusalem . . . that they should repent and turn to God, and do works meet for repentance (Acts 26:19,20).

Notice how the words agree completely with Joshua's "put away . . . and incline your heart."

The most amazing use of this word *repent* is seen in the book of Revelation. In chapters 2 and 3 the Lord Himself is writing the letters to the churches. When He writes to Ephesus He says, "Remember therefore from whence thou art fallen, and repent" (2:5). When He writes to Pergamos he says, "Repent; or else I will come unto thee quickly" (2:16). Writing to Sardis He says, "Remember therefore how thou hast received and heard, and hold fast, and repent" (3:3).

One final reference in the New Testament is most challenging. We are always ready to use Revelation 3:20 in our gospel preaching — "Behold I stand at the door and knock. . . ." This is actually part of the letter the risen Christ wrote to Laodicea. In quoting only verse 20 we miss the real point of the words of Christ. Look at verses 19 and 20 together. Christ says,

> As many as I love, I rebuke and chasten: be zealous therefore, and repent. Behold I stand at the door and knock. . . .

The invitation "Behold I stand at the door and knock," does not exist without the preceding "repent."

These references show to us the great importance the Bible places on the act and attitude of repentance. Notice that this is used not only for sinners but for Christians too.

Any response to God, or service for God, which does not come from a repentant and cleansed heart, is in danger of being weakened through the presence and power of sin. There is a tendency today to concentrate on the believing part of the gospel response, and to omit or soft-pedal the repenting part. Any response to Christ as Saviour which does not include a repentance from sin is in danger of producing a weak, colorless Christian witness, which will easily respond to the pull of the world once more.

Thus Joshua called the people to make a repentant choice. He wanted the quality of behavior which is detailed in II Corinthians 5:17:

> Therefore if any man be in Christ, he is a new creature: old things are passed away; behold, all things are become new.

He wanted the old things and the old ways to be put away and all things to become new as the people inclined their hearts unto the Lord God of Israel. Joshua 24:24 gives the response of the people to Joshua's call for a repentant choice: "The Lord our God will we serve, and his voice will we obey." Verse 25 continues, "So Joshua made a covenant with the people that day." How cleverly and positively Joshua had handled these disobedient people, taking them step by step and showing them so clearly what was involved in serving God. And how we need, so often, to be shown the same things in the same way so that our disobedient hearts may be brought to do real business with God.

Joshua had one more step to take before he ended this last great day in his life. "And Joshua wrote these words in the book of the law of God" (verse 26). In other words Joshua made it a *recorded choice*. He knew how fickle were these people, how short were their memories — so he recorded their choice, and he also put a great stone under an oak near the sanctuary of God.

> And Joshua said unto all the people, Behold, this stone shall be
> a witness unto us; for it hath heard all the words of the Lord
> which he spake unto us: it shall be therefore a witness unto you,
> lest ye deny your God.

There was thus the written word and the stone of witness to recall to their minds for all time the great decision made that day.

Many Christians find it a great help to make a record of their decision to turn to God and serve Him. There may be someone reading these words to whom God has spoken in the power of His Holy Spirit. You, too, may have made a real choice this day for God, realizing that it is a. responsible choice. You have also made it a repentant choice. It might help you if you made it a recorded choice as well, noting down in your Bible the day you did real business with God.

What we have discussed so far has dealt with the broadening detail of choice as Joshua brought the people face to face with the reality of their condition. It is also helpful to look for a moment not only at the detail of choice they made, but also at the depth on which they were challenged. This is shown for us in three stages. In verse 15 they were called upon *to choose*, in verse 23 to *incline their hearts*, and in verse 24 they promised *to obey*. Notice, in passing, that Joshua did not stop pressing the claims of God until he heard from the lips of the people their promise to obey.

We have seen in a previous chapter that the human heart is sometimes called the soul in the Bible. This is better recognized by us under the term human personality. This heart, soul, or human personality is divided into three areas — the mind, the emotions and the human will. One or two Scriptures will show this quite clearly. ". . . Wherefore think ye evil in your hearts?" Jesus asked. "Why reason ye . . . in your hearts?" (Matthew 9:4; Mark 2:8). The heart thus contains the area of thinking and reasoning — the mind. In Matthew 15:19 Jesus also spoke of the heart as the seat of evil emotions:

"Out of the heart of man proceed . . . murders, adulteries . . ."
And in John 14:1,27 He encouraged His disciples, "Let not
your heart be troubled . . . neither let it be afraid." The heart
thus contains not only the area of thinking but the emotions
also. But the heart is also the seat of the will. "Daniel pur-
posed in his heart" (Daniel 1:8). So the human heart — my
heart, my soul, my personality — consists of my mind, my
emotions and my will. If my whole heart is to be involved
in any decision I make, then it must be a decision that involves my mind (my intellect), my emotions and my will.

Joshua was calling his people to make a real decision for
God, and he revealed the depth of choice involving the whole
of the human heart by the three words he used: *choose* (verse
13), *incline your heart* (verse 23), *obey* (verse 24).

Choosing challenges the mind. The people had to reason
it through and make an intelligent response.

Incline your heart is a test for the emotions. Was there
real love in their hearts for God, a real hatred for the evil
ways they had been pursuing?

Obey is the final reaction of the will. Having reasoned
through the situation and put this alongside the love and devotion they had for Jehovah, the logical outcome was an act
of the will — a promise to obey.

This is how a real choice always has to be made. A people who are naturally disobedient, and who constantly limit
God by that same disobedience, must somehow be brought
to the place where they become vitally involved with God.
There must be not only an outward emotional response, but
an involvement of the whole human heart.

All this is applicable to us as Christians. So often our service for God is based on an emotional response. But we don't
sit down and reason it through, counting the cost of doing or
not doing the will of God. We somehow never come to the
place of taking the plunge and saying "I will, God helping
me. I will obey in thought, and word, and deed!"

CHAPTER 7

LIMITING GOD THROUGH FAILURE

IN THE PREVIOUS CHAPTER we considered the last great day in the life of Joshua, when he challenged the assembled people, and heard from their lips the final response: "The Lord our God will we serve, and his voice will we obey" (Joshua 24:24). It must have seemed so wonderful then, as the people looked back on their failure and forward to their future. "So Joshua let the people depart, every man to his inheritance" (verse 28), and off they went to enjoy all that God had promised them. What joy and hope must have filled the people's hearts — at long last the tragedy of Egypt and the wasted years of the wilderness were going to be vindicated.

The people went home with the promise of Joshua ringing in their hearts:

> The Lord your God, he shall expel them from before you, and drive them from out of your sight; and ye shall possess their land, as the Lord your God hath promised unto you (23:5).

He shall expel . . . and ye shall possess — this was the divine order for victory and success. God and God alone would do the expelling. Then they had to possess that which God had cleansed.

In order to back up the guarantee of blessing, Joshua had told them:

> And, behold, this day I am going the way of all the earth: and ye know in all your hearts and in all your souls, that not one thing

hath failed of all the good things which the Lord your God spake concerning you; all are come to pass unto you, and not one thing hath failed thereof.

Notice the fourfold use of the word *all* — all your hearts . . . all your souls . . . all the good things . . . all come to pass. How true, and what absolute confidence this should have inspired in all their hearts! This God who never fails was committed to the promise that he would expel . . . and they would possess.

So ends the book of Joshua. But the next book, Judges, tells the truth about what happened. Our passage in I Corinthians 10 reminds us constantly that we are to look at these people to see ourselves and to take warning. We can surely see ourselves in these people as they set out with high hopes to make a tremendous success out of life. Every promise they possessed is also ours to enjoy — only in a deeper sense, and with an added spiritual meaning. Some who read these words will be young in the faith. The thrilling excitement of what God has done for you at the Cross is still fresh in your hearts. Ahead of you lie new experiences and unknown adventures, and you are moving out, as the Israelites did, with a spirit of joyous expectancy. As you identify yourself with their adventure, see now the result of the quality of their faith.

And the Lord was with Judah; and he [Judah] drave out the inhabitants of the mountain; but could not drive out the inhabitants of the valley, because they had chariots of iron. . . .
And the children of Benjamin did not drive out the Jebusites that inhabited Jerusalem; but the Jebusites dwell with the children of Benjamin . . . unto this day. . . .
Neither did Manasseh drive out the inhabitants of Beth-shean and her towns . . .: but the Canaanites would dwell in that land. . . .
Neither did Ephraim drive out the Canaanites . . .; but the Canaanites dwelt . . . among them.
Neither did Zebulun drive out the inhabitants of Kitron . . .; but the Canaanites dwelt among them.
Neither did Asher. . . . Neither did Naphtali. . . . And the Amorites forced the children of Dan into the mountain: for they would not suffer them to come down to the valley.
— Judges 1:19,21,27,29,30,31,33,34

How quickly the whole picture had changed — nobody drove anybody out! Notice also that no tribe possessed their inheritance, they had to share it with those who were there before. Each tribe repeated, in a measure, the history of the nation when they first came out of Egypt. Under Moses the people came out of Egypt, but they never entered Canaan. They had enough faith to get out of Egypt, but not enough to go on into Canaan. Now each tribe had enough faith to go to their inheritance, but not enough to expel the enemy, and possess their possessions. What had gone wrong? Had God failed? After all, the promise was that "he shall expel . . . and ye shall possess." But no one was expelled and nothing was possessed.

We can find the answer to this great tragedy in Judges 2:1,2, where the account is given of a visit of an angel, or messenger, from God. Speaking for God he said:

> I made you to go up out of Egypt, and have brought you unto the land . . .; and I said, I will never break my covenant with you. And ye shall make no league with the inhabitants of this land; ye shall throw down their altars: but ye have not obeyed my voice: why have ye done this?

What a revealing challenge! "I will never break my covenant with you — but you have broken your covenant with me! You said, 'The Lord our God will we serve and his voice will we obey' " (Joshua 24:24), "but ye have not obeyed my voice." What a sad and searching question — "Why have ye done this?"

The answer is plain for all to see. God's people had been instructed to make no league, or peaceful agreement, with the inhabitants of Canaan; they had received the command to throw down all the heathen altars. But they had failed in both these areas. They did not want to see the end of the old sinful people and their wicked practices. They were more interested in arranging compromises than in carrying out commands.

I Corinthians 10 asks whether this is the way you began your Christian life. "If any man be in Christ, he is a new creature [creation]: old things are passed away; behold, all things are become new" (II Corinthians 5:17). But there are many of us who do not want the old things to pass away, and we would prefer that all things do not become new — just as it was in this story we are studying. The Canaanites and the Jebusites were far too interesting to be expelled completely. Their altars, their colorful pagan worship were much too exciting to be overthrown and discarded. But this initial step of compromise with the enemy left the seeds of future disaster buried in the soil of human experience, seeds which in later years produced crop after crop of temptation and tragedy and moral disaster.

Once again the children of Israel had failed in their promises, and their performance. As a result, God was limited. Joshua had assured them that God would expel their enemies and they would possess the land, but they were not willing to co-operate with God. As before, the flesh was lusting against the spirit, and all that emerged from the great "Operation Expel" was a miserable compromise which was unsatisfactory to everyone concerned.

God's reaction to their failure is seen in Judges 2:21,22:

> I also will not henceforth drive out any from before them of the nations which Joshua left when he died: That through them I may prove Israel whether they will keep the way of the Lord, to walk therein, as their fathers did keep it or not.

In this way God used their failure to test their faith. The situation produced by their disobedience was now permanent — there would always be the enemy resident in the land. But when they turned to God for strength and deliverance, in that measure they would be blessed.

This is a great truth to apply to our own hearts and experience. Many of God's people have failed in their personal living. Their lives, as a result, are shot through with failure and backsliding. The resulting weakness and defeat is obvious and cannot be denied. But there is no need to stay in the place of failure and defeat. God uses our failures to test our faith. If we accept failure as inevitable and incurable we condemn ourselves to a life of backsliding and barrenness. If, in spite of our failure, we come to God confessing our wretchedness, and seeking His cleansing and His power, then we turn our stumbling blocks into stepping stones. There is still hope of joy and blessing and fruitfulness for all who will see the promise of God and accept the victory which can be theirs.

The first need in the church today is not a widespread revival which will produce more Christians, but an inward revival which will produce better Christians. If those who truly profess and call themselves Christians were walking in all the joy of the Lord, and in the power of His Holy Spirit, they would demonstrate such a radiancy of daily living, that God would be unlimited in His capacity to use them. This is our greatest need — to demonstrate *life* through the indwelling Spirit of Christ.

This truth is hammered home again in I John 1:8,9:

> If we say that we have no sin, we deceive ourselves, and the truth is not in us. If we confess our sins, he is faithful and just to forgive us our sins, and to cleanse us from all unrighteousness.

If we will do one thing then God will do two things. If we confess our sin — not sit and moan about it, or be so introspective that we are constantly taken up with our failure — if we make a decisive move to have the thing dealt with, then God is just as decisive in His reaction. He is both faithful and just — faithful to His promises, and just with regard to His holiness and righteousness. God is always faithful and always just. The miracle of His grace springs from this eternal reality. Because He is both faithful and just He is able to forgive us our sins and also to cleanse us from all unrighteousness. He forgives our sins in relation to Himself in heaven. He cleanses us from the stain and the burden of sin in relation to ourselves.

This is a truth unknown to many Christians. They know their sins have been forgiven — that is their greatest joy. But they do not enter into the amazing fact that they are also cleansed, in God's sight they are clean and pure, ready and qualified to go on in His glorious service.

"I will not drive them out from before you; but they shall be as thorns in your sides." This was the Lord's response to His people's failure (Judges 2:3). Isn't this terribly true of some of us today? Our sins and our failures are allowed to remain and they become as thorns in our sides. The picture is of a man trying to make progress through a barren, desert-like country where the only thing that grows is thorny scrub. As he pushes his way through these bushes, he is constantly pricked and torn by the spikes and thorns piercing his clothing and his flesh. Progress is slow and almost impossible — one bush simply leads on to another.

But this need not be so. God's word is still faithful and just. He told the Israelites, "I will never break my covenant with you" (2:1). The words of Christ are still as precious and powerful today:

> Come unto me, all ye that labour and are heavy laden, and I will give you rest. Take my yoke upon you, and learn of me; for I am meek and lowly in heart: and ye shall find rest unto your souls. For my yoke is easy, and my burden is light (Matthew 11:28-30).

So far in our studies in this book we have linked I Corinthians 10 with Psalm 78, and have looked for examples and types of behavior which have "limited God." We have seen it in the lives of the children of Israel, then we have seen the same thing in our own experience. In contrast to this we can turn to I Thessalonians for another situation. Paul writes to the Christians in Thessalonica:

> And ye became followers of us, and of the Lord, having received the word in much affliction, with joy of the Holy Ghost: so that ye were ensamples to all that believe in Macedonia and Achaia.

Here we meet the same word that Paul used of the Old Testament characters — these people at Thessalonica were "ensamples" or examples to all that believe. But with what tremendous difference! In Psalm 78 we saw examples to be avoided. Here in I Thessalonians we are meeting a people whose daily living is so joyful, that it made them examples to be followed.

> We give thanks to God always for you all, making mention of you in our prayers; remembering without ceasing your work of faith, and labour of love, and patience of hope in our Lord Jesus Christ, in the sight of God and our Father (verses 3 and 4).

Just as in I Corinthians 10:1-4 the use of the word "all" gave us a picture of a 100 per cent church, so Paul uses the same word with regard to the Christians at Thessalonica — "we give thanks to God *always for you all.*" His choice of words indicates the preciseness of his feelings. Paul was much impressed and encouraged by *all of them always,* not by some of them sometimes! These words also indicate the quality of personal and corporate life which enabled the Holy Spirit to say that they were examples to all who believe.

There were three things that Paul remembered about the Thessalonians: their *work of faith,* their *labor of love,* their *patience of hope.* Now look at verses 8-10 and see what effect their faith produced elsewhere:

> For from you sounded out the word of the Lord not only in Macedonia and Achaia, but also in every place your faith to God-ward is spread abroad.

In every place your faith . . . is spread abroad. Not merely where Paul was, but everywhere in the Christian world of Paul's day people were talking about the church at Thessalonica, especially about their faith in God.

What three things had impressed the rest of the Christian Church?

> . . . how ye turned to God from idols to serve the living and true God; and to wait for his Son from heaven, whom he raised from the dead, even Jesus. . . .

They turned — they served — they waited. These three short

verbs give us the example for all to follow. If you compare these three actions that everybody noticed with the three things that Paul remembered, mentioned in verse 3, you will see how the Holy Spirit is especially emphasizing the example we have to follow.

Paul remembered first their *work of faith.* The first thing that the Thessalonians did was to *turn to God from idols.* This then was their work of faith — to turn to God from idols. Paul's second memory of them was of their *labor of love.* They had turned from idols *to serve the living and true God.* Paul's third memory was of their *patience of hope in our Lord Jesus Christ.* They were *waiting for God's Son from heaven.* These Christians at Thessalonica had a faith that worked, a love that labored, and a hope that was patient. What a challenge to us — especially if we contrast their success with the failure we have just witnessed in Judges 1 and 2.

The initial failure of the children of Israel, as detailed in Judges 1, was that they failed to drive out the enemy, and tear down their idols. They much preferred to compromise, so because of this first disobedience, everything else was doomed to failure. They never possessed their inheritance nor did they truly serve God. Instead, God was limited.

The initial success of the simple Christians at Thessalonica was that they turned to God from idols — which the Israelites did not do. Because of this first step, everything else became possible. This is where these two examples can speak to us at the same time — out of the mouth of two witnesses the truth shall be established. Big doors turn on little hinges, and so it is with our lives. Once we have firmly dealt with the "old inhabitants" in our life, then we have established the hinge upon which the door of Christian witness can turn. Instead of God being limited in our lives, we can go on, as the Thessalonians did "to serve the living and true God; and to wait for his Son from heaven."

CHAPTER 8

LIMITING GOD THROUGH PRIDE

ONE OF THE MOST TRAGIC FIGURES in the Bible is the man
known to us as Saul, the son of Kish. He could have been so
wonderfully used by God. Instead he completely limited
God by his arrogant pride and willful disobedience.

We met him first in I Samuel 9:1, 2. His father's name
was Kish. He was "a Benjamite, a mighty man of power."
Saul thus came from a wealthy, powerful family. From his
earliest days he would have enjoyed all the comforts and
pleasures of being a rich young man. Verse 2 describes him:

> a choice young man, and a goodly: and there was not among the
> children of Israel a goodlier person than he: from his shoulders
> and upward he was higher than any of the people.

What a wonderful start he had in life — a rich home, a powerful father, "tall, dark and handsome" — he had everything that
the world counts necessary for a successful, happy life.

Chapter 10 gives us details about his spiritual life. God
was moving in His divine counsels to call this young man
out to a position of national importance. Through a series of
unusual circumstances, God brought Saul in touch with the
prophet Samuel. Samuel, in a speech full of prophecy and
prediction, prepared the heart of Saul for the coming events.

> And the Spirit of the Lord will come upon thee . . . and thou
> shalt be turned into another man. . . . for God is with thee (verses
> 6,7).

Here, Saul came into contact with God in a new and living way. God was going to be with him in the person of His Holy Spirit. The lovely thing to notice here is the silence of Saul. These were events of major importance in his life. The challenge from God was almost overwhelming, and Saul's response was the silence of an obedient heart. Verse 9 records, "And it was so, that when he had turned his back to go from Samuel, God gave him another heart."

Now Saul's physical perfection was enhanced by the blessing of a changed heart. At this time in his history he must have represented man at his best. There was a quiet humility about him. When his uncle tried to find out what had happened, Saul was silent (10:14-16). His humility is even more apparent in verses 19-21. Samuel had called all Israel to present themselves for the choosing of a King. Saul was the man eventually selected — but "when they sought him, he could not be found." Imagine a presidential election with no sign of the successful candidate! Saul had hidden himself "among the stuff." Finally they found him and he stood higher than any of the people. "See ye him whom the Lord hath chosen," Samuel said, "that there is none like him among all the people?" "And all the people shouted, and said, God save the king."

Not only was Saul God's choice, he was the choice of the people also. So Saul, son of Kish, became King Saul of Israel, completing his all-around gifts of physical, moral and spiritual excellence. Here was indeed a King among men, God's choice!

Now that he was King, Saul was in a supreme position to honor God, to serve Him and to offer unlimited opportunity for God's will to be done. But from this moment on, there creeps in little by little a spirit of disobedient pride. What could have been a life marvelously used by God became a life where God was limited in every area. God's next step was to test Saul in two special ways — first by sacrifice. After the joy and thrill of the coronation came the tragedy of calamity. The Philistines gathered themselves to make war on the new king of Israel, and their armies were formidable. Verse 5 of chapter 13 records the chariots and horsemen and "people as the sand which is on the sea shore in multitude." God was now going to test the faith of this young king of Israel. Samuel told Saul to wait in Gilgal for at least seven days, and he promised that before the end of the seventh day, he would return. When he came, he would make supplication to God, offer the burnt offering and peace offering, and God would give them victory. So Saul was left on his own with his small army — but with the promise of God.

What followed next was agony for Saul. As each day passed the forces of the Philistines increased. He could see them from the mountain tops gathering in the valley below — more chariots, more cavalry, more infantry. Not only could Saul see this, but his own army watched with increasing fear and apprehension. Soon the Israelites began to slink away and "hide themselves in caves, and in thickets, and in rocks, and in high places, and in pits." Some even left the country. The remainder followed Saul trembling.

Saul waited as Samuel had instructed him — one, two, three . . . six days. But still there was no sign of Samuel. Finally the seventh day dawned and Saul could stand it no longer. His eyes were now off God, and fixed on the impossible situation around him. In desperation he called for the sacrifices and offerings and, against all the law of God, he who was not a priest usurped that authority, and approached God in his own strength to offer the sacrifice. Just as he finished making the offering, Samuel arrived as he had promised — but it was too late.

"And Samuel said to Saul, Thou hast done foolishly" (verse 13). Saul had been tested by sacrifice but he had failed miserably. God could have won a great victory that day, but He was limited by the pride and disobedience of Saul. God had made him King, but he made himself a priest. In doing so he sinned and forfeited the right to receive the blessing of God. Saul had the promise of all the blessing, but he couldn't wait for God to bring it in His own way.

Our New Testament passage challenges us once more. Is this the way you and I behave? We have been blessed far more than ever Saul was. He had the Spirit of God upon him, but we have the Spirit dwelling in our hearts and lives. We are told continually to wait on the Lord and to trust in Him, but how often, when faced with problems, do we rush out and try to solve the whole thing in our own strength, forgetting to wait for God? So often it could be said of us, *Thou hast done foolishly*.

Then God tested King Saul again not only in respect to his sacrifice, but with regard to his faithful, obedient service.

> Samuel also said unto Saul, The Lord sent me to anoint thee to be king over his people, over Israel: now therefore hearken thou unto the voice of the words of the Lord (15:1).

Samuel went on to give strict instructions to Saul, telling him to gather an army and lead an expedition against the Amalekites. These people had been a source of constant trouble to Israel, even when they were in the wilderness. If they were allowed to continue they would be like a malignant cancer in the life of Israel. So Saul was commanded to perform spiritual surgery and destroy the Amalekites completely — people and possessions. The command was inclusive:

> Now go and smite Amalek, and utterly destroy all that they have, and spare them not.

So Saul departed to perform the will of the Lord, but when he arrived at the place of operation he completely disobeyed the instructions given to him by Samuel. Some of the people he killed, some he kept alive. Concerning the cattle,

all that was good, [he] would not utterly destroy them: but everything that was vile and refuse, that they destroyed utterly (verse
9).

Saul interpreted the will of God to please himself, and in so
doing he failed once more. God's response was immediate.
Speaking to Samuel He said:

> It repenteth me, that I have set up Saul to be king: for he is turned
> back from following me, and hath not performed my command-
> ments. And it grieved Samuel; and he cried unto the Lord all
> night (verse 11).

When he was challenged by Samuel, Saul demonstrated
his departure from God by his lies and excuses.

> I have performed the commandment of the Lord. And Samuel
> said, What meaneth then this bleating of the sheep in mine ears,
> . . . and Saul said, They have brought them . . . to sacrifice unto
> the Lord, thy God (verses 13-15).

He blamed the people for the decisions he had made, and
offered God as an excuse. Samuel had to cut Saul down to
size, to tell him exactly where he stood. But Saul continued to
blame the others, and to suggest that the animals were a
sacrifice to God. Samuel replied with these magnificent words:

> Hath the Lord as great delight in burnt offerings and sacrifices,
> as in obeying the voice of the Lord? Behold, to obey is better
> than sacrifice, and to hearken than the fat of rams (verse 22).

Samuel then went on to pronounce the sentence of God
upon this proud rebellious man.

> For rebellion is as the sin of witchcraft, and stubbornness is as
> iniquity and idolatry. Because thou hast rejected the word of the
> Lord, he hath also rejected thee from being king.

Saul's rebellion and stubbornness had limited God, and as a
result, Saul was finished. The chapter continues with Saul
still on the defensive, still excusing his rebellion, still refusing
to bow his proud will. "I have sinned," he acknowledges to
Samuel, "yet honour me now, I pray thee, before the elders
of my people, and before Israel" (verse 30). A sinner seeking honor for himself and his sin!

What a challenge to us today — *to obey is better than sacrifice*. How often we will make sacrifices to excuse our lack of obedience, giving our money, our time, when all the while what the Lord really wants is our genuine obedience to what He has commanded us. Notice that this is how we can limit God. In the eyes of the world our contributions and enthusiasm may rank high as good examples of Christian living and giving — and all the time what the Lord really wants is to hear us say, "Yes, Lord, Thy will be done!"

From this time on, Saul was God's man no longer. He sat on the throne and wore the crown, but "Samuel came no more to see Saul until the day of his death" (verse 35). God left him to perish. I Samuel 26:21 reports Saul's evaluation of his life in one of his more honest moments toward the end of his life: "Behold, I have played the fool, and have erred exceedingly." Gone is the boasting pride. He looks back over his life and sees himself as he really is. Saul, who began with so much, is now ending with so little. It could have been so very, very different, but he limited God for the sake of rebellious pride. As I think of this man, my own heart is challenged and humbled. "Let him that thinketh he standeth take heed lest he fall" (I Corinthians 10:12).

I Samuel 16 goes on to tell the lovely story of how God chose the man he wanted to replace Saul. Samuel, still mourning for Saul, was commanded by God to go to Bethlehem to find Jesse and to anoint one of his sons to be the next king over Israel. Saul was still on the throne, but in one sense he was gone, because Samuel was mourning him as God was quite prepared to ignore him. Samuel's reaction to God's command was one of fear. Saul would kill him. But God sent Samuel under his care and protection. Samuel was sent to anoint the next king, but he did not know which son was to be the chosen man. The account of the choice is an excellent story, full of good teaching for us.

Samuel's arrival caused great consternation in Bethlehem — he was an awesome personality, but he reassured the people and was soon engaged with the family of Farmer Jesse. The Bible gives the names of several of Jesse's sons, making the story much more meaningful. Names in the Bible, both of people and places, have a special significance. (The most precious name of all is Jesus, meaning Saviour — "thou shalt call his name Jesus: for he shall save his people from their sins," Matthew 1:21). A person's name was often a guide to his character or work; a place's name often described it accurately. So it was with the sons of Jesse.

The first son interviewed by Samuel was the oldest, a man named Eliab. His name meant "God is my Father," indicating a man whose outward characteristics were those of holiness and religious behavior. When Samuel saw this man, the oldest, with his air of holiness, he immediately thought that this was God's man. After all Eliab was godly and holy in appearance, so different from what Saul was in his rebellious pride. But Samuel was corrected by God by these wonderful words:

> Look not on his countenance, or on the height of his stature; because I have refused him: for the Lord seeth not as man seeth; for man looketh on the outward appearance, but the Lord looketh on the heart (verse 7).

Eliab looked holy and handsome and godly and good, but that was only on the outside. Inside God saw failure, and sin.

The next son to be considered was a man named Abinadab (verse 8). This name means, "My Father is noble," and indicates a person with dignity of walk and nobility of personality. Samuel's reaction to such a man would be obvious. Here was a man who looked like a king! Eliab looked holy, but this man looked kingly — surely this was the man whom

God had provided. But this wasn't God's man either. God looked within his heart and saw nothing noble or kingly. So Abinadab was sent on his way.

The third son to pass before Samuel was "Shammah." This name means "valor" or "courage" — to use a good modern expression "Tough Guy." Here was a muscle-man, big and powerful. As Samuel gazed on his rippling muscles, he would remember the need of a fighter to lead the people against the Philistines. Here was just the man for the job. But when God looked at his heart, he found nothing that was brave or true, and Shammah joined his brothers.

Verse 10 tells us that Jesse introduced all his sons until he had made seven men to pass before Samuel, but none were chosen. At this point there was a breakdown in candidates, and Samuel asked Jesse if these were all his sons. Possibly Samuel thought he had misinterpreted God's will. Jesse replied that these were all the grown-up sons, but there was still one youngster on the hills looking after the sheep. Samuel asked to see this final member of the family, and so the servants went and called for David. "Now he was ruddy, and withal of a beautiful countenance, and goodly to look to."

As David drew near to Samuel in all the fresh, clean vigor of a teenager, God spoke to Samuel, "*Arise, anoint him: for this is he.*" The youngest and least important was God's man, David the shepherd boy. The lovely part of this story is to realize the meaning of the name David — *Beloved.* The other names all drew attention to the outward characteristics of the men concerned, but "David" denotes an inward conviction. Here was one who loved God above all else. This was the boy who later could write:

> I will love thee, O Lord, my strength. . . . The Lord is my shepherd; I shall not want. . . . I will extol thee, O Lord. . . . Bless the Lord, O my soul . . . I love the Lord (Psalms 18,23,30,103,116).

This was the boy who grew up to be God's wonderful king, so human, so humble, so ready at all times to serve the Lord.

All that Saul might have been came true in David; all that Saul never was, was manifest in this boy who grew up to honor God in all things.

Chapter 16, which we have just considered, shows us God choosing a man. Chapter 17 shows us God using a man. It begins with a story of abject defeat. Saul is there with all the army of Israel, but they are being defied by one Philistine, Goliath of Gad. We all know the story of David and Goliath, but there are interesting details which illustrate our present subject, "Limiting God," and which contrast for us the characters of Saul and David.

Goliath's cry was not for a battle but for a man: "I defy the armies of Israel this day; give me a man, that we may fight together" (verse 10). This was the job for Saul. He was the tallest in Israel, he was the leader. But "when Saul and all Israel heard those words of the Philistine, they were dismayed, and greatly afraid" (verse 11). Eliab and Abinadab and Shammah, David's brothers, were there, but they too were greatly afraid. Verse 16 tells us that Goliath "drew near morning and evening, and presented himself forty days." Saul and his army were being brainwashed by this ugly brute. Eighty times they listened to his taunts, powerless to resist him. Once, Saul waited seven days for the Philistines. Now he waited forty days — but God had left him and his army to handle the situation, and his waiting was purposeless.

Then verse 17 tells how Jesse sent David to the place of battle to greet his brothers. He arrived just as the Israelites were moving to the place of battle, and he shouted and cheered them on. But suddenly they all stopped and listened once more to Goliath. As Goliath finished his challenge the men of Israel fled from before him. David stood and watched an army running away in utter confusion, demoralized and dispirited. He saw King Saul run — and Eliab and Abinadab and Shammah.

David was fresh to the battlefield. His mind was unperturbed by Goliath. His days had been spent with God, taking care of his flock, and so he gazed in puzzled wonder. He began asking questions and making suggestions, expressing his willingness to tackle Goliath. His words reached the ears of Saul who sent for him. David's words in verse 32 are most challenging — "Let no man's heart fail because of him; thy servant will go and fight with this Philistine."

Now the two men face each other. Saul and all Israel are brainwashed, and Saul speaks of David's utter inability to meet a man trained for battle, a man who was nine feet, six inches tall! David recounts what God had done for him in previous struggles with a bear and a lion, and then he proclaims in absolute faith "the Lord that delivered me out of the paw of the lion, and out of the paw of the bear, he will deliver me out of the hand of this Philistine." The others were all looking at the same problem — Goliath. Saul and all Israel were saying, "Look at him, look at his size, his power, look how much bigger he is than we are!" David was saying, "Yes, but look how much smaller he is than God!" Saul, the failure, was helpless and hopeless. All he could do now was to continue to limit God. David, God's new man, was confident — all his hopes were centered on God.

Saul next attempted to clothe David in the usual armor for battle. He was concerned with making David strong on the outside. But David took the armor off and pushed it away with these pointed words: "I cannot go with these; for I have not proved them" (verse 39). But he had proved God, and so he was going with God.

The reality of David's faith stands out as he replied to the taunting of Goliath: "Thou comest to me with a sword, and with a spear, and with a shield: but I come to thee in the name of the Lord of hosts, the God of the armies of Israel, whom thou hast defied" (verse 45). David had his priorities right. Goliath wasn't fighting David, but God! So that David could confidently say, "This day will the Lord deliver thee into mine hand; and I will smite thee" (verse 46).

Here was faith supreme, yet all the time up on the hillside, Saul and Eliab, Abinadab and Shammah trembled with fear. These four men had all been candidates for kingship. One was even then wearing the crown. But all had failed, and the proof of their failure was their fear. God was right when He refused holy Eliab and dignified Abinadab and tough Shammah. Their qualities were only on the outside after all. But David's love was his joy and his strength, and he proved it out there, on his own, alone — with God.

The rest of the story is well known — the choosing of the five smooth stones, the use of the simple sling, the crashing fall of Goliath, and the sudden bravery that filled the fearful hearts of the men of Israel. And all because a teenager saw God in the situation!

We often fail to appreciate the matter of the five smooth stones. Why did David choose five when he only used one? Was he unsure of his aim? We can find the answer, remarkably clear, in II Samuel 21:18-22. The events recorded in this chapter are, of course, much later than those of our story. Saul is dead and gone, and David is king. There were more battles with the Philistines. Saph was killed in one (verse 18) — he was "of the sons of the giant." In another battle in the same place, one of David's men slew "the brother of Goliath the Gittite" (verse 19). In verse 20 we learn that there was still another battle in Gath, and another man of great stature defied Israel. "He also was born to the giant," and was slain by the son of Shammah (David's nephew). Verse 22 concludes:

> These four were born to the giant in Gath, and fell by the hand of David, and by the hand of his servants.

Here we learn that Goliath had several brothers. The possibility was that when Goliath fell in combat with David, his brothers might have rushed to tackle David. If they had, David had stones for them — however many giants came that day David was ready for them. Here was the perfect example of God being unlimited in the devotion of a teenager.

The great thing to realize here is that David had enough resources to meet every possible situation. It is a wonderful thing to learn that a situation only becomes a problem if I don't have sufficient resources to meet it. If I have the resources, then the situation becomes an incident. So for David, the situation wasn't a problem, only an incident. He had all the resources he needed in God.

What a contrast these two make — Saul and David. Yet Saul could have enjoyed all the blessing that David enjoyed, if he had only humbled his will and yielded his heart.

Do you have any Goliaths in your life just now? Situations, or people, or circumstances, that have been defying you for days or weeks or months? Have you been brainwashed into accepting defiance and defeat as the normal life for you? David's God is your God. David could say, "I will fear no evil: for thou art with me." Can you say that? Can you go forward into the situation recognizing the presence of Christ and believing with childlike faith that "greater is he that is in you, than he that is in the world" (I John 4:4). In this way your situations will cease to be problems and simply become incidents, under the almighty hand of God.

CHAPTER 9

LIMITING GOD THROUGH LAZINESS

THERE IS A LOVELY STORY of a mother putting her three-year-old daughter to bed. She tucked her in, kissed her good-night, then went downstairs to her sewing. The house was quiet and all was peaceful — for a while. Suddenly there was a resounding thump from the bedroom, silence, then the loud wail of a sleepy, frightened child. The mother rushed up-stairs to find her daughter lying on the floor, crying.

In a few moments peace was restored and the little one was back in bed. Just before she left the room, the mother asked, "Sweetheart, however did you come to fall out of bed?" "I 'spects I fell asleep too near the place where I got in," was the reply.

And that describes one of the biggest problems in the church today — Christians who fall asleep too near the place where they get in. In a very real sense this is why so many "fall out" with each other. It is very rewarding to meet a church where the Gospel is faithfully preached and where souls are truly saved and blessed; this is exactly how the church should operate. But the problem develops when, in such churches, there is a settling down to the satisfaction of being saved, when the general pattern of thinking is "Good! We have heard the Gospel, we have trusted Christ, our sins are forgiven, we are on our way to heaven—we have arrived!

108

This is it — now we can settle down." The initial occupation with Christ slips away, and instead of going on and growing up in the faith, there begins a busy occupation with "things," and with the fringe non-essentials of the Christian faith. People become slack and the vision begins to fade. We become members of an organization, and lazy in living. So we limit God in our personal lives, and in our church life.

In II Kings 2:1-14 we have a story which has a tremendous message for the present-day church. It concerns two men — Elijah, the old prophet of God, and Elisha, the younger man standing on the threshold of life. Elisha makes a series of simple decisions, but without realizing that the decisions he makes that day are going to affect the rest of his life. Elisha lived to serve God for fifty-five more years. Nearly two generations of successful service for God came as a result of these decisions. But it could all have been so different, so useless, if he had chosen a wrong way, an easy way. God was unlimited in what He could do in and through the life of Elisha — there were miracles and marvels and mysteries. But it all began when a young man made a right decision.

God can use His word to speak to our hearts as we consider this story. Someone who reads these words may be in a similar position. You, too, may be on the threshold of wonderful experiences with God. If you choose aright, the whole future may be a joyous unfolding of the will of God in your life. On the other hand, you may be settling down, satisfied and at ease, lazy and heedless — and God will be limited once more. Our limitation of God doesn't depend upon age, whether we're too old or too young; or on sex or profession, whether we're able and gifted. It depends upon one thing only — whether we are prepared to go on with God.

As the story opens in II Kings 2 we find the stage is set for a tremendous occasion. Elisha had been with Elijah for several years as his personal servant, seeing and hearing all that the old man did. Elijah was a rough and tough man of God. He seemed to lack the quality of gracious kindness in all his dealings with people. In this story there is an abruptness and almost lack of concern in the language he used to Elisha. However, he knew he was soon to depart this life, and he used the events to test the heart and intentions of Elisha. Elijah is always moving on, but always encouraging Elisha to settle down and "tarry here." The value of the story is to see and understand the reactions of the young man to these deliberate temptations to "take it easy."

The story is concerned with four separate places, Gilgal, Bethel, Jericho and Jordan. Each was a very significant place in the history of the children of Israel. Elijah and Elisha are on the move (verse 1). Elijah knows his destination and the dramatic events which will happen there, but he sets himself to dissuade Elisha from accompanying him. We meet them first at Gilgal. Elijah says, "Tarry here, I pray thee; for the Lord hath sent me to Bethel." There was no need for Elisha to continue the journey. He was going to end his friendship with Elijah soon, so here was a good place to settle down.

What I want to do now is to share with you the thoughts that could easily have come to the mind of Elisha, as he was invited to settle down in Gilgal. Elisha was, in a sense, a theological student, preparing for the ministry, and as such he would be very familiar with the history of his people and with the historical significance of Gilgal.

When he thought of Gilgal he would immediately remember the events we have recorded in Joshua 5. Gilgal was the place of beginnings. When the children of Israel at last moved out of the wilderness and into the land of promise, Gilgal was the first place they came to. So in one sense, Elisha was being tempted to settle down in the very beginning — just like many of us do. We get into the land of promise, we are saved and blessed — and then we settle down because we have arrived!

Gilgal was also the place of *separation,* for it was here that "the Lord said unto Joshua, Make thee sharp knives, and circumcise again the children of Israel the second time." Circumcision was the sign of separation. As the people were about to move into association with other nations, they were to be set apart for God. Gilgal was also the place of *satisfaction* (Joshua 5:10-12), for it was here that they kept the passover, and ate for the first time the food of Canaan along with the manna.

In verses 13-15 we have the wonderful story of how Joshua met "a man over against him with his sword drawn in his hand." This man had awesome words to say: "As captain of the host of the Lord am I now come. . . . Loose thy shoe from off thy foot; for the place whereon thou standest is holy." This was none other than the Lord Jesus Himself meeting Joshua. The *man* could not have been an angel, because He demanded worship. He was divine. God is a Spirit and "no man hath seen God at any time" (John 1:18), so it was not God the Father, or God the Holy Spirit, but God the Son.

Think what this meant now to Joshua. Having met this glorious captain of the host of the Lord, Gilgal was not only a place of *separation* and *satisfaction,* but a place of *unlimited strength.* Notice, however, that it was a place of the promise of unlimited strength. It was a place of beginnings where so much blessing and strength were promised. But if we settle down here, all we have are promises — nothing is ever proved. No victories were won at Gilgal, no progress was made. It was a place for feeling happy and hearing promises. No wonder Elisha refused to tarry at Gilgal. He wanted to go on and experience more and more of the goodness of God.

Unfortunately many Christians today have settled down

in Gilgal. We have arrived, we have the blessing, we have the promises. So we settle down and sing wonderful hymns about the promises of God — but we never go on to prove the promises. We are happy to quote and re-quote the words of our Lord Jesus: "Lo, I am with you alway, even unto the end of the world" (Matthew 28:20). But then we go out and live as if not a word of it was true.

Gilgal would bring other pictures to the mind of the young man Elisha. He would think of another young man named Saul. In our previous chapter we looked at Saul and David. If you check in I Samuel you will see what a significant part Gilgal played in the life of Saul. He was crowned king there by Samuel (I Samuel 11:14,15). Gilgal was thus the place of beginning for the young man Saul. As we have seen, I Samuel 13 records the story of how Saul was tested when Samuel delayed his coming. Gilgal was the place where Saul could not wait for God, where in his fear and anxiety he offered the burnt offering and the peace offering himself. So Gilgal was the place where Saul not only began but where he also failed.

Chapter 15 tells the story of how Saul was sent to deal with the Amalekites, to perform spiritual surgery for God. He failed once more to do the will of God, and Samuel was commissioned by God to tell him that God was finished with him. Verse 12 tells how Samuel rose early to meet Saul in the morning. He looked for him at Carmel and eventually found him at Gilgal. So that it was at Gilgal that Saul began as God's man, that he failed in sacrifice, and that he was judged by God.

No wonder that when Elijah said to Elisha, "Tarry here at Gilgal," he was not in the least interested. What a place, what memories, what a warning to any young man! And what about us? We settle down where we begin, we fail to go on in the things of God. Where we settle, there we fail, and there we finish — still in Gilgal!

Elijah then went on with Elisha to Bethel. We learn from verse 3 that sons of the prophets were living at Bethel. This would be a school or training center for young men. Once again Elijah spoke. "Elisha, tarry here, I pray thee; for the Lord hath sent me to Jericho." Here was another invitation to give up "going on" and to settle down. There were other young men there. Elisha could join them, and busy himself with their daily activities.

But what memories would the name Bethel bring to the mind of the young man Elisha? He would think surely of the story told in Genesis 28 about another man who was "going on" and who was also at the beginning of his new life. Jacob was on his way to his Uncle Laban's at Padan-aram. He had deceived his father Isaac, incurred the hatred of his brother Esau, and now he was running away from the unhealthy and dangerous situation his behavior had brought about.

Verse 10 records how Jacob began his long weary journey. At night fall he found a place to sleep and "tarried there all night." While he slept he had a dream which is recorded in verses 12-15. God appeared to him and told him what He was planning for his future. When Jacob awoke, "he called the name of that place Bethel" (verse 19). Bethel was the place where a young man dreamed a dream of what would happen in years to come. Elisha was invited to tarry at Bethel, to join the other dreamers and think about the future. But Jacob didn't stop at Bethel, and neither did Elisha.

The tragedy is that many young Christians are quite happy to tarry at Bethel and dream dreams about their future. It is wonderful to think of what might be, and to dream about how lovely it would be if God really took your life and used you, and sent you forth in His name. But if all we do is sit and dream about the future, we limit God. All the great missionary enterprises today, whether at home or abroad, spoken, printed, on radio or TV — all these had their beginning in the dream or vision of a waiting, watching Christian. Proverbs 29:18 says that *"where there is no vision, the people perish."* Where there is a vision there are infinite possibilities for future blessing — so long as we don't tarry at Bethel, and limit God.

Bethel would also call to mind the story of another young man who was beginning a new life under new conditions. In I Kings 11 we have the story of the death of the great King Solomon, the beginning of what could have been a tremendous life for a man named Jeroboam. God had planned to divide the kingdom of Solomon after his death. His son, Rehoboam, was to be left with the one tribe of Judah and the remaining tribes were to be formed into the separate Kingdom of Israel. God sent a prophet named Ahijah to give this information to Jeroboam.

> Thus saith the Lord, the God of Israel, Behold, I will rend the kingdom out of the hand of Solomon, and will give ten tribes to thee. . . . And I will take thee, and thou shalt reign according to all that thy soul desireth, and shalt be king over Israel (verses 31,37).

Here was a tremendous promise from God, and all for one man. Chapter 12 goes on to report how this promise came true, just as God had said. But the real lesson for us is what happened in the life of Jeroboam after he was made king.

He had heard and received the absolute, sure promise of God — "I will take thee and thou shalt reign." But "Jeroboam said in his heart, Now shall the kingdom return to the house of David" (12:26). He didn't believe that God could keep it up! He reasoned that when the people of his new Kingdom went to worship God at the Temple in Jerusalem they would change their minds, and return to Rehoboam, who would kill him. So Jeroboam thought up a wonderful way in which he could get what God had already promised. There was no need for his plan. It showed an absolute lack of faith in God. But like so many of us he tried to help God out of His difficulties!

> Whereupon the king took counsel, and made two calves of gold, and said unto them, It is too much for you to go up to Jerusalem: behold thy gods, O Israel, which brought thee up out of the land of Egypt. And he set the one in Bethel. . . .

Then Jeroboam ordained a feast and "made priests of the lowest of the people." He built up a new order of worship all centered in Bethel — an order "which he had devised of his own heart" (verses 31-33).

From this chapter on, the Bible refers to Jeroboam as "Jeroboam the son of Nebat who made Israel to sin." Bethel was the place where one young man dreamed dreams, and where another young man schemed schemes. No wonder that when Elijah invited Elisha to join the other young men also at Bethel, he replied, "As the Lord liveth, and as thy soul liveth, I will not leave thee" (II Kings 2:4). Elisha was more concerned with a living Lord than with a place of promise!

Verses 5 and 6 of II Kings 2 tell us what happened when the two travelers came to Jericho. Here was another group of the sons of the prophets. They also came to Elisha to cause him distress of soul. And once again the old man Elijah told his young companion to tarry at Jericho and join the others.

Elisha is now faced with another and more subtle temptation. Jericho was a beautiful place, much to be desired. As he thought back on the history of his people, one memory of Jericho would stand out, above all others. Jericho was the place where Joshua led the people to victory. The children of Israel never forgot the story — how they marched round this impregnable city so strong in its walled defenses, how on the seventh day at the given signal they all shouted and the walls of Jericho fell flat, and they marched in and sacked

the whole city. This was their first great victory. In fact
Jericho was known especially for this one incident. Jericho
was the place of past victory.

Many Christians today, especially the older ones, tarry
at Jericho, the place of past victory and talk about the good
old days — and nothing else! Jericho should have a special
meaning for Americans — the name means "The City of
Palms," and the town was noted for its famous spring. So
that Jericho carries the image of Palm Springs — the lovely
place to which people retire in the winter. When the weather
is unpleasant in the other states it is lovely to settle down in
Palm Springs, to enjoy the warm sun, and the absence of bitter winds, frost and snow.

What a picture Jericho brings to our minds — "Tarry thou
in Jericho" — the place where you can retire and talk about
past victories. And this is exactly what some Christians do
in a spiritual sense. They are not so young as they used to
be, and following the pattern of the social and industrial
world, they start to take life easy and move into a state of
spiritual retirement. We need to remember that God has no
old-age pensioners. Nobody is ever retired in God's service.
All that God does is to "re-tire" us, so that we are capable of
further service for Him.

We could do with a new organization in our country
along with Youth for Christ — "Age for Christ." There are
so many jobs which can only be done by those who have
years and experience on their side. Thank God for all the
older Christians in our churches today. But too many of these
dear people have written themselves off as being no good to
God. They are each sitting in their own special Jericho, they
love to talk about what God did for them and through them
in days gone by, but they are limiting God by tarrying there.

There is work for older people as well as for younger ones.
There is need for persistent prayer warriors, for others who

can visit shut-ins and bring them the comfort of God. Even bedridden patients can develop a special ministry of prayer and intercession. Letter writing can be a means of challenge for God and comfort to those in need. In all these no great physical strain is necessary, just a quiet willingness to "go on" with God. Remember that Moses was eighty years old when he *began* his life's work for God!

Elisha was now committed to going all the way with Elijah. Leaving Gilgal and Bethel and Jericho behind them, they journeyed on until they came to Jordan. Notice now what Elijah did to this young man who insisted on going all out for God. He took him out of the promised land, out of Canaan, and into the wilderness. Not only did he lead him to the wilderness — he left him there. True service for God began with Elisha alone in the wilderness. Elijah was taken, but his mantle — the symbol of his power — remained. If Elisha was ever going to be of any service for God, he had to cross his own Jordan.

Any Christian who means real business for God must come to this experience in his own life. He must see himself in his own true relationship to the plan and will of God. This was no casual day in the life of Elisha — this was *the day*. On this day's decision hung the effectiveness of the next 55 years.

So Elisha stood all alone by his own Jordan. Once he had crossed it he would be back in Canaan, not as the friend of Elijah this time, but as the prophet of God. He was still holding the mantle of Elijah, the symbol of his power. But never before had Elisha called upon God. He had had no direct personal contact with God, only through Elijah. Now was his moment to step out in faith, in a faith he had never known or used before. "Where is the Lord God of Elijah?" he cried. At the same time he smote the waters as Elijah had done. God answered his question by revealing His power (verse 14), and Elisha went down into Jordan.

In a much later day, Jordan was the place of baptism, where many went down into the water to demonstrate a break with the old life, and the beginning of a new experience — a dying to self and a rising to a new life. This was the experience of Elisha. He came into living vital contact with God. He went down into Jordan symbolizing his break with all the past. He came out of Jordan on the Canaan side — God's man for ever more. He had refused to tarry at Bethel or Gilgal or Jericho. He wanted God's best, and he was prepared to pay the price — a recognition of the presence and power of God, and a dying to his own life, hopes and ambitions.

The Lord Jesus put this picture into words in Matthew 16:24: "If any man will come after me, let him deny himself, and take up his cross, and follow me." All the elements of the story in II Kings 2 are to be found in these words. *If any man will come after me* — this is the initial challenge of the Christian life. After whom, or after what am I going? Or am I content to be what I am? Elisha was not content to tarry anywhere. He continued following, leaving behind the ease and the pleasure, seeking only God's best.

Let him deny himself. This puts the finger on the root of all weakness — myself. The self which demands a constant recognition, whether it be good or bad, holy or hopeless, self has to be denied, as Elisha denied himself.

And take up the cross — this is the very center of the operation. It is good to pause a moment and consider the words, *the cross*. What was the purpose of a cross? In many churches the cross is a thing of precious beauty made of gold and jewels which calls for worship and adoration. But the cross was not a thing to be worshiped. Some people wear a cross as a symbol of their faith. This is good in a way, but the cross is not an ornament to be worn. Others speak of "taking up the cross," referring to the difficulties and problems they have in their daily lives — their illnesses, their physical weakness, their job, an unpleasant husband or wife. But this is not what Christ meant — nothing so small and mean as that.

The cross in our Lord's day was used for one purpose only — to die on! It was an ugly, cruel thing, an instrument of punishment which meant death to the one who hung on it. The only effective way to *deny self* is to *take up the cross* and "die" on it. This is the faithful preaching of Romans 6.

> . . . we . . . are dead to sin (verse 2). . . . we are buried with him by baptism into death [as Elisha was in Jordan] (verse 4). . . . our old man [the self life] is crucified with him, that the body of sin might be destroyed (verse 6).

The natural reaction to this teaching is to say, "Yes, but I'm very much alive. I'm not dead. My 'self' is a real problem!" Verse 11 teaches us how to deal with this problem:

> Likewise reckon ye also yourselves to be dead indeed unto sin, but alive unto God through Jesus Christ our Lord.

It is a day-by-day, and moment-by-moment reckoning that I have no need to sin, to indulge self, to lose my temper. I count on the fact that Christ has already dealt with my self life. Jesus Christ not only died for my sins, He died for *me*, in my place. When Christ died, I died. "I am crucified with Christ . . . the Son of God, who loved me, and gave himself for me" (Galatians 2:20).

The great word in Romans 6:11 is *reckon*. Its companion is found in verse 13:

> Neither yield ye your members as instruments of unrighteousness unto sin: but yield yourselves unto God, as those that are alive from the dead, and your members as instruments of righteousness unto God.

It is the great word *yield*. I *reckon* myself dead to sin, and I *yield* myself as an instrument — a tool or weapon or implement — unto God. I take my hands off my own life, and allow

God to take me and use me as He wills. This is exactly what Elisha did. He "died" in Jordan and came out "alive" for God.

The last of Jesus' statement to His disciples is, *Follow me*. This is the obvious next step to yielding my life to God. It is this *following* which many earnest Christians overlook. They make sincere decisions for Christ and dedicate their lives to Him — and then expect to have gloriously changed lives overnight. They forget that we grow in grace, we don't suddenly blossom out into full-grown Christians overnight. It is a slow steady growing in grace, a slow steady following Christ. I must moment-by-moment reckon myself dead unto sin, and moment-by-moment yield myself unto Christ. When this is my constant aim in life, there will be no limiting of God, no laziness towards God, but a walking by faith and a growing in grace.

CHAPTER 10

LIMITING GOD THROUGH IGNORANCE

I SPOKE RECENTLY at a high school in England, confronting the students with the reality of God. In Britain the law of the land states that each school day must begin with an act of worship and that there must be instruction in Religious Knowledge. This means that there is great opportunity for the truth to be presented; conversely there is also an opportunity for the non-believing teacher to present a warped version of the Christian faith.

The school to which I went had three full-time teachers of Religious Knowledge, and all three were sincere, committed Christians. It was because of their love for Christ that I was invited. They warned me to expect real opposition to what I said, not only from the students but from other members of the staff.

It is a strange fact that, in some places, the church has succeeded mainly in arousing a spirit of rebellion and resistance in the young people. I talked about this feeling with the students, and it was obvious in many cases that they had chosen simply to ignore the church and all that it stood for. They complained of the dreary services, of the fact that most of the congregation were older people who, in some cases, almost resented the presence of teenagers. They commented on the irrelevance of what the ministers preached. They all agreed that there was no "life" about the whole thing — it was a weekly "performance."

Now we realize that this is not true of every church. But it does show one important fact. These young people and many others like them have thrown God overboard, not because of antagonism, but because they are utterly ignorant of what the truth really is.

As I listened to their honest comments I had to agree with them on many things. It was like this when I was a teenager. Services were dull and automatic, and so completely irrelevant to my life as a young man. I remember making the rounds of the various denominations seeking satisfaction, and in the end giving up the whole thing in disgust.

During my visit to the school I had many opportunities to speak to the students honestly as man to man. I knew that most of these young men and women were ignorant of the truth. They were passing a judgment on Christianity based, not on God and His glorious provision, but on the performance of an organization.

During assembly I spoke to the whole school about what the Bible and human experience had to say about them — the students. We saw from I Thessalonians 5:23 ("I pray God your whole spirit and soul and body be preserved blameless") that each human being is a threefold entity of spirit, soul and body. We examined this idea more closely to see how true and logical it is. Our bodies we know quite well, especially in the area of games and sports and eating! Our souls are provided for through the medium of the school. The soul includes the mind, the emotions and the will, all of which we educate at school. Then we thought about the human spirit. This idea was new to many of them, I discovered as I went from group to group later on in my visit. We thought of the human spirit as that unique part of man which makes him *man*. It is the God-shaped blank in every life that never finds true satisfaction until there is a real personal involvement with God.

It is the spirit that differentiates man from the animal world. No one has ever seen an animal pray. They have no inner urge to worship or placate a supernatural being outside themselves. Animals, for all their interesting ways, do not possess the capacity to know God. Like us they have a body with which they are world-conscious. Like us they possess, in a lesser degree, a soul — that is, a capacity to use a mind, to show emotions, to exercise a will. But there the likeness ends.

I told the school about my oldest son who is a missionary with the Sudan Interior Mission in Southern Ethiopia. He has recently moved into a new area to begin a completely new pioneer work. It is estimated there are half a million tribespeople there in one densely populated area. Yet until a few months ago they had never heard the name of Jesus. In spite of this ignorance concerning Jesus, these people are all involved in worship to their own gods.

This characteristic of man is true wherever explorers have penetrated. Wherever human beings are found, they are worshiping some form of a being outside themselves. Man is a worshiping animal. Through the human spirit, man is God-conscious.

We thought of the sense of "seeking" that fills the life of a growing teenager. He is always seeking something, someone, somehow, somewhere — something to fill the growing sense of emptiness. We recognized that the biggest need in the life of a teenager is for something to overcome his sense of insecurity. So much of the trouble caused by teenagers today is the outward expression of this inward seeking. Because young people have so much freedom, the areas of expression are many and varied.

I pressed home the point that only one thing can fill that

God-shaped blank — God Himself. We considered the ways in which many teenagers express themselves in this search for *Life*. The desire for new experiences leads many to indulge in sex and drink and drugs — all associated in a way with the adult life for which they are reaching. But such experiences can never fill the emptiness. They only serve to increase the guilt which in turn increases the need for inward peace and satisfaction. Finally, we considered that the whole purpose of the Bible was to show us how God can fill that blank in the person of His Son.

This was information new to many of the students. It was logical, it explained their own natures and need, and they listened with increasing interest. Later on, when I went to speak to smaller groups of the students, one question was asked repeatedly: "If this is so, how can I fill this God-shaped blank? How can God become real in my life?" This gave me the opportunity to present Christ as God's answer to man's need. They asked and they listened — and, strange to say, there was no antagonism or rebellion. They were hearing now, not about a God as represented by a denominational group, but a God who had become suddenly relevant to their own experience.

I have been working with young people for over thirty years, and I have always found it to be true that once teenagers see the relevance of God and Christ to their particular needs, there is no immediate rebellion or resistance. Not every one will accept Christ, but at least, they meet Him as the one who still says, "Come unto me, all ye that labour and are heavy laden, and I will give you rest" (Matthew 11:28). They are no longer ignorant of who God is, or what He can do for them and through them.

This sense of ignorance affects not only the teenager. Many Christians have a vision which is weak and dim because of their ignorance of God and His purpose. They never truly apprehend what the Christian faith really consists of. They have only a hazy idea of its nature. They are standing in the right place, and looking in the right direction, but the mists of ignorance and uncertainty produce a vagueness which lessens their capabilities. And so they limit God.

Consider with me now, one of the basic concepts taught in the Bible concerning God and Christ. Without a true appreciation of this truth any Christian life and witness will be the poorer. We began this book by looking at the failures of the children of Israel when they came out of Egypt. Now let us see what God was thinking and planning for them.

After He had brought His people out of Egypt and given them the Ten Commandments, God spoke to Moses about His plans for the redeemed people. Exodus 25:1-9 records the words. The people were to bring offerings of various kinds, but they were to be given willingly. No one should be compelled to give. The offerings were for a specific purpose: "And let them make me a sanctuary; that I may dwell among them" (verse 8).

Stop for a moment and realize the greatness of this concept. God's first thought for His redeemed people was that He might dwell among them. The chapters that follow are all devoted to telling of the glories of the Tabernacle, the tent where God would dwell. The idea is repeated again in chapter 29:45,46:

> And I will dwell among the children of Israel, and will be their God. And they shall know that I am the Lord their God, that brought them forth out of the land of Egypt, that I may dwell among them: I am the Lord their God.

Consider again these words, *I brought them forth . . . that I may dwell among them.* Remember that, at this time, these children of Israel were nothing but a gang of freed slaves. There was probably much about them that was unlovely and unpleasant. Many were uncouth and ungracious.

Yet it was among this type of people that God was planning to live and make His presence known. He would not wait until the conditions were better and the people were improved. God's desire was to dwell among His people.

Exodus 35 describes the beginning of the construction of the Tabernacle. There is a continual emphasis on the qualifications necessary for a giver or a worker.

> Whosoever is of a willing heart, . . . (verse 5). And every wise hearted among you shall come, . . . (verse 10). And they came, every one whose heart stirred him up, and every one whom his spirit made willing . . . And they came, both men and women, as many as were willing hearted . . . (verses 21,22). And all the women that were wise hearted did spin with their hands (verse 25).

The results of the people's willingness is seen in chapter 36:7: "For the stuff they had was sufficient for all the work to make it, and too much."

The last two chapters of Exodus are concerned with the completion and assembly of the Tabernacle ". . . as the Lord commanded Moses," is the constantly recurring phrase. Chapter 40:33 says, "So Moses finished the work." Then God moved in, as He said He would. His glory filled the place and no one was able to remain within the Tabernacle. Exodus ends with the visible symbols of God's presence constantly in evidence.

> For the cloud of the Lord was upon the tabernacle by day, and the fire was on it by night, in the sight of all the house of Israel. . . . (40:38).

God was with His people. God's *presence* was with them, to carry out God's *plan,* by God's *power.* God was in the midst, but He was in control.

The rest of the Old Testament is the history of Israel's response to the presence of God. God was there in the Tabernacle. Later He was in the Temple — but always God's presence for God's plan by God's power. Sometimes the peo-

ple responded to God's presence with love and joyous obedience, especially in the days of David. When this happened
they had peace and blessing and prosperity. Sometimes the
people turned away from God to serve Baal and other false
gods. Then they experienced tragedy and failure and even
captivity, until they repented and cried again to God for His
presence, His plan and His power — for God in the midst, in
control.

This, then, is the truth set forth throughout the Old Testament. Let us see the same truth in the New Testament.
John 19 records the awful suffering of Christ and His death
on the cross. "He bearing his cross went forth into a place
called . . . Golgotha: where they crucified him, and two other
with him, on either side one, and Jesus in the midst" (verses
17,18). Here we have the story of *redemption*. Notice the
fact recorded about Calvary: *Jesus in the midst*. The same
great truth of the Old Testament was being worked out in
the New Testament. God in the midst — His presence, His
plan, His power. This time, "God was in Christ, reconciling
the world unto himself" (II Corinthians 5:19).

Never think, for one moment, that the Jews finally cap-
tured Jesus and succeeded in doing to Him all that they
desired. It is thrilling to realize that, all the time, Jesus
was in control. Matthew 26:47-56 tells how the multitude
came to the Mount of Olives to capture Jesus. In verse 51
we read how one of the disciples (Peter) drew his sword and
started fighting. Jesus stopped him, explaining, "Thinkest
thou that I cannot now pray to my Father, and he shall pres-
ently give me more than twelve legions of angels?" A legion
consisted of 6,000 men, so that twelve legions would be more
than 72,000 angels — all waiting for Jesus to call on their
mighty power. But He never did. He was in control all the
time. Even on the cross it was *Jesus in the midst*. As in the

Old Testament, our response to this truth is the measure of our faith and love towards God.

John 20 records the triumph of the Resurrection, culminating in the excitement of verses 19 and 20:

> Then the same day at evening, being the first day of the week . . . , came Jesus and stood in the midst, and saith unto them, Peace be unto you. . . . Then were the disciples glad, when they saw the Lord.

Here is the same truth once more. The joy of the *Resurrection* was *Jesus in the midst*. His presence brought the joy. Verse 21 records His plan: "As my Father hath sent me, even so send I you. . . . Receive ye the Holy Ghost." Their response to this glorious reality was again the measure of their faith.

This is seen in the following verses 24-29 where we read of Thomas, called Didymus. He was absent on that wonderful night. For him there was no Jesus in the midst. His response to the wonderful news was, "Except I shall see . . . I will not believe." Eight days later they were in the same room, "and Thomas with them: then came Jesus . . . and stood in the midst, and said, Peace be unto you" (verse 26). Once more Jesus was in the midst. This time Thomas met his risen Lord and from his lips came those wondrous words: "My Lord and my God."

In the last book of the New Testament, John, now the aged apostle, is still concerned with the same truth. He was in the Spirit on the Lord's day when he heard behind him a voice like a trumpet. As he listened the voice began to tell forth great words of revelation.

> And I turned to see the voice that spake within me. And being turned, I saw seven golden candlesticks; and in the midst . . . one like unto the Son of man (Revelation 1:12,13).

Here again is the same phrase — the truth of *revelation* is *Jesus in the midst*. Here most definitely is His presence. His plan is seen in 22:16: "I Jesus have sent mine angel to testify unto you these things in the churches." His power is evident in every chapter.

Revelation 5 takes us to the throne room of heaven and gives us another view of Jesus. We read of the strong angel "proclaiming with a loud voice, Who is worthy to open the book, and to loose the seals thereof?" (verse 2). John was distressed because "no man in heaven, nor in earth, neither under the earth, was able to open the book" (verse 3). Then one of the elders told him to cease crying for some one was worthy and able.

> And I beheld, and lo, in the midst of the throne, and of the four beasts, and in the midst of the elders, stood a Lamb as it had been slain (verse 6).

On the throne of heaven was the Lamb of God. Once more Jesus Christ is in the midst. This time He is *reigning*.

The glory of heaven is the Lamb in the midst. No wonder we read in verses 11 and 12:

> And I beheld, and I heard the voice of many angels round about the throne and the beasts and the elders: and the number of them was ten thousand times ten thousand, and thousands of thousands; saying with a loud voice, Worthy is the Lamb that was slain to receive power, and riches, and wisdom, and strength, and honour, and glory, and blessing.

What a glorious scene that will be, when the One who was *in the midst on the cross* will be *in the midst on the throne*. And again the great truth is proclaimed. His presence tells forth His plan as he opens the seven seals. His power is the power of heaven in all its fullness.

It will be a wonderful day when we all get to heaven. But before all the wonder of heaven is experienced, there is another glorious day to come. We read about it in I Thessalonians 4:16, 17.

> For the Lord himself shall descend from heaven . . . and the dead in Christ shall rise first: then we which are alive and remain shall be caught up together with them. . . .

Our supreme joy and delight is that we shall "meet the Lord in the air." This time He is *returning*, and the hope of the Second Coming is *Jesus in the midst*. It will surely be His presence that calls us; His plan for us will be fulfilled; His power is the means whereby all these blessed experiences come true. No wonder we are to "comfort one another with these words."

The references to Jesus in the midst which we have been examining, have all been connected with events of climactic importance. There is one other reference which is especially lovely, because it involves each one of us. "For where two or three are gathered together in my name, there am I in the midst of them" (Matthew 18:20). This doesn't refer to some great event scheduled for the future, but to the gathering of Christians for prayer. It is the same Jesus, in the same place — *in the midst*. His presence is our only reason for gathering. His plan is that which we seek as we bow in prayer. His power is what we count upon as we close our prayer with the words, "through our Lord Jesus Christ. Amen."

So in both the Old and New Testaments the truth is set forth — God in the midst; God in control. But now we need to be involved, each one personally, as we take this same truth and apply it to our own lives. II Corinthians 13:5 switches the spotlight from the Bible to the believer:

> Examine yourselves, whether ye be in the faith; prove your own selves. Know ye not your own selves, how that Jesus Christ is in you, except ye be reprobates?

In this tremendous challenge, see the threefold emphasis: *yourselves . . . your own selves . . . your own selves.* The proof of the reality of my faith is not my words but the witness of the presence of Christ. A Christian is a person like you and me who has Jesus Christ's presence in him — *Jesus in the midst*. We have seen enough now in the chapter to know that He is there for one specific purpose. He has not come primarily to make us holy or respectable or happy — these may come later. If Jesus is in the midst, then He is there to *control* through His person, His plan, His power — that is, if we are aware of the basic truth of God's word.

Earlier in this chapter we said that "many Christians have a vision which is weak and dim because of their ignorance of God and His purposes." Ignorance of the vital truth that God must be in control produces a weak, feeble witness. This is the ignorance that limits God.

In conclusion, let us look at I Corinthians 6:19,20. In this passage we are brought full circle back to the establishing of the sanctuary in Exodus with which we began this chapter.

> What? Know ye not that your body is the temple of the Holy Ghost which is in you, which ye have of God, and ye are not your own?

In the book of Exodus, we saw the willing hearted and the wise hearted providing the means whereby God could dwell in the midst of His redeemed people. Now the truth is complete. We Christians do not provide the material for the temple, we — our bodies in all their weakness — are the temple.

The children of Israel, we saw, among whom God dwelt, were not rich or important or especially selected. They were just a bunch of slaves redeemed from Egypt. So it is with us. When we accept Christ as our Saviour, He comes to dwell in our hearts in the person of His Holy Spirit. He comes to us just as we are. There is no waiting until we are worthy. If He did wait He would never come at all! His desire is to dwell in our hearts and to make our bodies, individually, the temple of God.

Now we can begin to understand that our own personal history will parallel the history of God's people in the Old Testament. When they recognized God's presence to control

— His presence, His plan, His power — then they enjoyed blessing and peace and success. God was not limited. Instead His will and His word went forth with power. Conversely, when they forsook God and went their own way they ran into problems, enemies, defeat, and even captivity.

This is the promise of the pattern for your life. If you will recognize your body as God's temple, and give to Him that which is rightly His (not only by creation but by purchase — "for ye are bought with a price"), then you, too, will enjoy blessing and peace and success. But, if you choose to retain control of your own life, for good reasons or for bad, in the measure that you retain control in that same measure will you run into problems, enemies, defeat, and even captivity. This is the basic law of God:

> Be not deceived; God is not mocked: for whatsoever a man soweth, that shall he also reap. For he that soweth to his flesh shall of the flesh reap corruption; but he that soweth to the Spirit shall of the Spirit reap life everlasting (Galatians 6:7,8).

Ignorance is no excuse for failure, but it is a sure way to limit God in all His purposes. How wonderful it would be if some of us realized, perhaps for the first time, what is really involved in being a Christian. If we choose to retain control of our lives then we will continue in our weak, sickly, powerless living. There will be no joy in our hearts, no blessing to other people, and God will be limited once more. But if we act now on the truth we have heard, then blessing will be inevitable.

CHAPTER 11

LIMITING GOD THROUGH IMMATURITY

To THOSE OF US WHO KNOW and love the Lord, the Bible is very precious. We accept it as the inspired Word of God. We remember that many men and women in years past have died for this book, for their faith in it and for their attempts to promote its outreach. Some of us, however, fail to realize that the Bible is not only inspired in the writing; it is equally inspired in the selection of the books included in it.

Several books mentioned by name in the Bible were equally inspired with the Biblical books, but we have no copy of them today. I Chronicles 29:29, referring to the acts of David the King, mentions three books: the book of Samuel the seer, the book of Nathan the prophet, and the book of Gad the seer. Today we have only the book of Samuel in our Bible, but the others were equally inspired. II Chronicles 9:29, in summing up the life of Solomon, tells of three books in which "the acts of Solomon, first and last" are recorded. It details the book of Nathan the prophet, the prophecy of Ahijah, and the visions of Iddo the seer. All these were accepted books of God in those days, but we have no copy of them today.

In the New Testament, Colossians 4:16 refers to the epistle to the Laodiceans, a letter from Paul which existed in the early days of the church and was used for guidance and instruction — but we have no copy of it in our Bible today. It is an interesting thought that God was just as careful to see what was kept out of the Bible as He was to give true guidance concerning what was included. Why choose the letter to Colossae and not the one to Laodicea? When we compare these two places the question becomes even more pressing.

Colossae at the time of the early church was a little unimportant place, a small town in the province of Asia, tucked away in the Lycus Valley. It was a little "nowhere" inhabited by little "nobodies." Laodicea, on the other hand, was an important center for commerce. The church there would have been larger, more influential and, in one sense, more important. Then why choose Colossae and omit Laodicea? By our standards today the affairs of one of our large churches would be much more important than those of some tiny church tucked away on a side street. If we think in terms of our own experience we can call to mind important churches that draw crowds and have a far-reaching ministry. There are smaller places we pass on the road which mean nothing in our Christian experience. This is how it was with Colossae.

The obvious conclusion is that God must have something of real importance to say to us if He included the letter to this tiny church. The Colossian epistle has a tremendous message for every church today, for it deals with the subtle ways in which a church can be true and successful and yet be limiting God.

Many churches today are active, well organized, with excellent programs and a successful youth work. Yet somehow they are not making that quality of impact on the world around as could be expected. Many ministers and church officials are conscious of areas of weakness in the outreach of the church, and are earnestly seeking to meet this by special programs, by reorganization, by developing new and attractive techniques. But these miss the mark and the church still continues to limit God. This was the condition of the church at Colossae. The letter that Paul wrote, inspired by the Holy Spirit, was God's answer to the need of that church. So this letter has a message for every church today. Here is a diagnosis of weakness, with the true remedy to restore power and effectiveness.

If we continue with our study of this letter we find important information not only about Colossae but about the persons involved in the writing. Chapter 4:18 tells us that it was written by Paul and that he was in prison at the time. We find also that Paul had never been to Colossae and had never met the people. Chapter 1:4 and 7 explain that his knowledge of the place and the people was only by hearsay. Chapter 2:1 emphasizes the point that the Colossians had never seen Paul "in the flesh." The other man involved in this story is Epaphras, a Colossian (4:12). He had preached the message of the Gospel to his fellow townspeople (1:7), and he was the one who, humanly speaking, caused the letter to be written.

At the time of the writing of this letter, Epaphras was with Paul in Rome. He had brought to Paul a full report of the state of the church. The information gave Paul great joy. But then, as Epaphras continued his report, Paul was quick to see the weakness in the church and the possible danger which would develop if action was not taken to deal with the situation promptly and effectively. We do not know what it was that Epaphras said, but we do have Paul's written response to the report. Paul's diagnosis, under the inspiration of the Holy Spirit, is the supreme value of this letter to us today. He is careful to analyze the areas of weakness and to give the kind of teaching and advice that will equip the church for a fuller and more effective outreach for God.

We need to bear in mind that most of the Christians at

Colossae were Gentiles. This is evident from 1:27 and 2:13, where Paul addresses them specifically as Gentiles and as uncircumcized. (In a sense most churches today are like the Colossian church — we have not seen Paul and we are mostly Gentiles.) Paul begins by praising them for the good things he has heard concerning them (1:1-8). Later on he is going to write them strong words that will challenge them and revolutionize their faith, but to begin with he recognizes them as "faithful brethren" (verse 2), and speaks of their "faith in Christ Jesus, and of the love which ye have to all the saints" (verse 4), and of their "love in the spirit" (verse 8).

A study of the letter shows that Paul had analyzed the church's problem into three areas. First he warned them about having *other priorities* in their faith. These people had been pagans for most of their life. They had been accustomed to worshiping many gods and spiritual powers — a god for every area of human life and experience. As Christians, they were still caught by a similar attitude. Paul writes:

> Let no man beguile you of your reward in a voluntary humility and worshipping of angels, intruding into those things which he hath not seen, vainly puffed up by his fleshly mind (2:18).

Jesus Christ was important to them, but He wasn't all-important. They were worshiping angels and spiritual powers as well as Christ. There were other things and beings in their lives that demanded top-line importance. They had other priorities besides Christ.

What was true in the church at Colossae is often true in our churches today. We can get our priorities wrong. We, too, can be involved with other priorities that detract from Christ and inevitably limit God in His outreach. For these people at Colossae, Jesus Christ just wasn't big enough in their knowledge and estimation to cope with the needs in their busy lives. Their God was too small, and so they brought in angels to help Him out. As verse 19 says, they were not holding the Head from which all the body by joints and bands having nourishment ministered, and knit together, increaseth with the increase of God.

Because they were not "holding the Head" alone, they were suffering from spiritual malnutrition. Spiritual malnutrition is one of the prevailing weaknesses in the church today.

Paul goes on to show that because they had priorities other than Christ they were in danger of having *other philosophies* apart from the truth of God.

I write like this to prevent you from being led astray by someone or other's attractive arguments. . . . Be careful that nobody spoils your faith through intellectualism or high-sounding nonsense. Such stuff is at best founded on men's ideas of the nature of the world, and disregards Christ! (2:4,8; Phillips).

If I reject the teaching and authority of the Word of God then I must produce a substitute from somewhere. So it was with the Christians at Colossae. Having a Christ who was too small, they also had a Word of God that was too small. They were dabbling in philosophy and "high-sounding nonsense" to support the new approach they had in Christian worship.

If Christ is not recognized in all that He truly is, and if other experiences and alternatives are brought in, then there must, of necessity, be the downgrading of the Word of God and the introduction of intellectualism and philosophy to support the new steps being taken. We can be absolutely certain that "such stuff is at best founded on men's ideas of the nature of the world, and disregards Christ."

Continuing his analysis of the situation Paul went on to warn against *other practices* for holiness. This is the natural outcome of the first two weaknesses. If Christ is not given His rightful place in my life, then I will be taken up with other less important details. Not having the fullness of Christ I will need to draw on men's ideas and philosophies for my wisdom. Finally I will need to draw on other practices for

my walk and my Christian holiness. To the church at Colossae
Paul wrote because they were concerning themselves about
the outward appearances of holiness,

> . . . don't let anyone worry you by criticizing what you eat or
> drink, or what holy ways you ought to observe, or bothering you
> over new moons or Sabbaths. All these things have at most only a
> symbolical value: the solid fact is Christ. . . .
> So if, through your faith in Christ, you are dead to the principles
> of this world's life, why, as if you were still part and parcel of
> this world-wide system, do you take the slightest notice of these
> purely human prohibitions — "Don't touch this," "Don't taste that,"
> and "Don't handle the other?" "This," "that," "the other" will all
> pass away after use! I know that these regulations look wise with
> their self-inspired efforts at worship, their policy of self-humbling,
> and their studied neglect of the body. But in actual practice they
> do honor, not to God, but to man's own pride (2:16,17,20-23;
> Phillips).

The Christians at Colossae were trying to develop a quality
of holiness which, ultimately, would resound to the glory of
man.

We must learn at all costs that true holiness is nothing
less than the life of Christ being made manifest through the
mortal bodies of the believer (II Corinthians 4:10,11). Holiness begins on the inside and works its way out through the
yielded life — day by day.

This then was the threefold problem that Paul recognized
in the Colossian Church. His purpose in writing to them was
to deal with this situation spiritually, intelligently and effectively. Notice that Paul does not attack them or blame them
or condemn them. His whole approach is positive not negative. He begins his answer to their need by a glorious declara-
tion of the supreme lordship of Christ. In their eyes Christ
was insufficient to meet their needs and unable to handle
their problems. Paul exalts and magnifies the Lord Jesus. He
shows that Jesus is Lord by His person — who He is; by His
power — what He did; by His place — where He is.

Jesus Christ, Paul states,

is the exact likeness of the unseen God — the visible representation
of the invisible; He is the First-born — of all creation (1:15; Amplified).

This is who He is. There is no need for other priorities — Jesus
Christ is Lord over all. All that they worshiped at Colossae
was subservient to Christ. In these days of declension from
the truth of God's word this is something which should char-
acterize and underline all our thinking — the supreme lordship of Christ.

Paul continued to magnify Christ by speaking of His
power.

> For by him were all things created . . .: all things were created
> by him, and for him: and he is before all things and by him all
> things consist (1:16,17).

This is what Christ did in creation. Notice, incidentally, the
phrase "by him all things consist," or *are held together*. I
was speaking some weeks ago to a brilliant nuclear-physicist
who is a dedicated Christian. He told me how his research
work strengthened his faith. As he went further and further
in his studies of the atom, he was constantly meeting the fact
that there was an unknown, unseen power which literally
held the atom together and consequently held this very world
together. He said that for him this was the significance of
the words "by him all things consist." Not only did Christ
create the world but He holds it together by His own power.

Still speaking of the power of Christ, Paul detailed in
verses 20-22 of chapter 1 the other aspect of His work:

> And, having made peace through the blood of his cross, by him
> to reconcile all things unto himself . . . in the body of his flesh
> through death.

Here we have the amazing contrast in the glorious work of
Christ. To create, He only had to speak, but to redeem, He
had to die. Because of all the stupendous work that he accomplished He is Lord of all. This is something we need to
bear in mind constantly. We can be so impressed by men

who nibble at the fringe of power, that we lose sight, as the Colossians did, of the One who is the source of all power.

The third point Paul emphasized was that Christ was Lord by His place — where He is. The Colossians had an exalted Christ but, along with him, they had other supernatural beings. But Jesus Christ is

> the head of the body, the church: who is the beginning, the first born from the dead; that in all he might have the preeminence (1:18).
> [He] is the authority over all authorities, and the supreme power over all powers (2:10; Phillips).

There is no one to challenge His position. He is supreme. We need to emphasize this truth in these days. In some of our churches Jesus is numbered with the great men and with the great teachers of the world. He stands with Buddha, and Confucius and Mohammed. His words are great words, to which we ought to listen. But this is not enough. Jesus is "over all, God blessed for ever," (Romans 9:5), and His words are to be obeyed, not merely discussed.

We have looked at Paul's analysis of the Colossian church's problem, and his answer to meet the need. Another great ministry of this letter is the application Paul makes of his own Gospel. The Gospel they had heard and believed came by way of Epaphras who was a faithful minister of Christ. But the ultimate result of Epaphras' preaching was to leave them — as we have seen — incomplete in their appreciation of Christ and His truth. Paul writes to the Colossians about his commission — he was made a minister of the Gospel, "to fulfill the word of God" (1:23,25). It was his privilege to complete or fully expound the Gospel which he describes as "the mystery which hath been hid from ages and from generations, but now is made manifest to his saints" (verse 26). Paul uses the most extravagant language to focus attention on "the mystery" — God wants to make known "the riches of the glory of the mystery . . . which is *Christ in you, the hope of glory*" (verse 27).

The exceeding wonder and glory of the gospel message is that the Christ who died for me on the cross now lives in my heart and life in the person of His Holy Spirit. This is the culminating truth in all the treasure house of God. It was this truth that the Colossians did not know, and their ignorance led to their failure. In the church today, this blessed mystery of the indwelling Christ is often an unknown truth, and ignorance of it leads to failure and to our limiting of God.

Now, note carefully how Paul continues in verses 28 and 29. Having established this central truth of *Christ in you* he continues in the same sentence,

> Whom [Christ] we preach, warning every man, and teaching every man in all wisdom; that we may present every man perfect in Christ Jesus.

Notice the threefold aim in Paul's preaching: warning, teaching, presenting. It was a personal ministry — Paul uses the phrase "every man" three times in the one sentence. Verse 28 is one of the most important verses in the Bible for preachers and evangelists. Paul — the greatest preacher, teacher, missionary and evangelist — here gives us the secret of his ministry.

Paul began by warning every man. In common with every other New Testament preacher he preached warning and judgment to all. There are preachers today who would rather woo than warn, whose message is all of love and never of judgment. Paul was a preacher who warned.

Paul's second purpose in his preaching was to teach every man, a purpose often overlooked in some churches. In recent months I have had people come to me at different times and in different places, each with the same remark: "I'm not condemning our Pastor. He is a real man of God and he preaches the Gospel faithfully — but that's our trouble. Every Sunday morning he preaches 'Come to Jesus and get your sins forgiven.' He does the same thing every Sunday night and if he speaks during the week he has the same message. It is wonderful to hear the simple Gospel, but we want to be taught from the Word of God." Here were fine men of God who missed out on Paul's second aim — not only warning, but teaching the Word. In my years of preaching and traveling I have always found that if a minister preaches and teaches the word of God with authority, the people will come, regardless of what denomination he may represent!

Paul had one final object in all his warning and teaching: "that we may present every man perfect in Christ Jesus." Remember that Paul was preaching and teaching "the riches of the glory of the mystery . . . which is Christ in you." So his ultimate aim would be a man or a woman perfect in Christ. The word "perfect" here really means *mature*. Paul was aiming at producing mature believers. He was not interested only in saving sinners, but in teaching them so that they might become mature. This maturity was one based on a conscious sense of the indwelling Spirit of Christ. This is what the Colossian church lacked. It had no mature believers — only saved sinners untaught in the Word of God. That is why it was a problem church with other priorities, other philosophies and other practices.

This is what so many of our good evangelistic churches lack today — mature believers, with a maturity based on the conscious daily sense of the indwelling Spirit of Christ. In so many evangelical churches there are only saved sinners who are untaught in the Word of God. How we thank God for the fact that the Gospel is preached and that souls are saved. But you cannot build a strong church out of people who are just babes in Christ. You must go on to teach them and lead them to maturity based on the fact of the indwelling Christ — *Christ in you.*

We ought to challenge ourselves with the question, "Am I a mature Christian? Is my maturity based on the sure sense that Christ indwells me and that my life is the·vehicle for His will?" Some of us will have to be honest and admit that while we may claim to be mature, it is a maturity based on wrong priorities. Do I consider myself mature because of the length of my Christian experience, or because of the office I hold in the church, or because I have gray hair, or for some other reason which has somehow satisfied me up to now? Some men I know are rich and hold high office in the church — but they are far from real maturity. It isn't a case of Christ being made manifest through them but of self, self, and more self! Conversely, I have met some wonderful young people who love the Lord with a pure heart, whose lives are crystal clear in their devotion to Him, and who have yielded their whole beings to His service — such are mature in all the fullness of Christ.

The word "perfect," meaning *mature* is an interesting word which is used elsewhere in the New Testament with remarkable significance. In Matthew 19:16-22 there is the story of the rich young ruler who came with his great question to Jesus: "Good Master, what good thing shall I do, that I may have eternal life?" Here was a young man who possessed everything else in life — wealth, position, youth, social standing — but who wanted the greatest thing of all, eternal life. As the Lord Jesus spoke to him, he was able to show the good quality of his life. Yet he was not satisfied. "What lack I yet?" he asked.

> Jesus said unto him, If thou wilt be perfect [there is the same word once more — if thou wilt be mature] go and sell that thou hast, and give to the poor, and thou shalt have treasure in heaven: and come and follow me.

Maturity, as described by Christ, is based on a relationship, not with the world and its possessions, but with the person of Christ. This is what Paul was saying in his letter — maturity is based on a personal, intimate relationship with Christ.

The sequel to the story in Matthew is well known. When he heard the challenge of Christ, the rich young man went away sorrowful. He wanted maturity, but not at that price. You will notice that Christ did not call him back, or lower His terms to accommodate the young man. God has no bargain basement! Whosoever will may come, but we come on God's terms. We can have all the blessings of God to the full, on God's terms. Maturity is only mine when I yield my life to Christ and recognize that He indwells me to use me for His own purposes.

We meet the same word in Ephesians 4:11-13 where Paul writes about the special workers God has given to the church, whose ministry is to teach and lead us

> till we all come in the unity of the faith, and of the knowledge of the Son of God, unto a perfect man, unto the measure of the stature of the fulness of Christ (verse 13).

The Amplified New Testament has an excellent translation here:

> that [we might arrive] at really mature manhood — the completeness of personality which is nothing less than the standard height of Christ's own perfection — the measure of the stature of the fulness of the Christ, *and* the completeness found in Him.

Here again Christian maturity is shown as a living relationship with the risen Christ in all His fullness.

Colossians 4:12 is an interesting verse, because it contains the prayer of Epaphras, the man who had first spoken to these people in Colossae, who had established the church, and who had come to Paul with the problems of his people.

> Epaphras, who is one of you, a servant of Christ, saluteth you, always labouring fervently for you in prayers, that ye may stand perfect and complete in all the will of God.

Epaphras always labored fervently in prayer, but for just the one thing — that his people might "stand perfect and complete in all the will of God." He realized that only one thing was missing in that church. It wasn't torn with sin and strife like the church at Corinth. There is no sign or reference to evil or wickedness. They just lacked the one great truth that could change their weak witness into a dynamic outreach for God. They needed to know the living Christ in such a way that they were truly mature.

Isn't this the prayer, the one prayer, needed for many of us and our churches in this day? How about having special specific prayer meetings for the maturity of believers? Perhaps if we prayed more for the believers we would have greater blessing in the outreach of the Gospel. This is what Epaphras prayed for.

Finally, Epaphras prayed that, being mature his people might then be "complete." This word "complete" is a lovely picture word in the Greek text. It means "completely filled," and was often used to describe a sailing ship driving before the wind with every sail up and billowing out as the wind caught and filled every inch of canvas. What a glorious picture of a Christian, a mature Christian, filled with the fullness of Christ, surging on in the Master's business. There is no canvas below decks. Every sail, every means of fullness, is committed to the power of the driving wind. There is no clatter of machinery, no man-made power being used, only the sound of the wind blowing "where it listeth, and thou hearest the sound thereof, but canst not tell whence it cometh, and whither it goeth: so is every one that is born of the Spirit" (John 3:8).

So often our churches are like quiet harbors where the ships lie each one tied to his own mooring place. The sails are there, but they are stowed away below decks. There is no driving before the wind on urgent business, taking rich cargoes to needy people — just a gentle rocking to and fro at the mooring. When the tide comes in there is a gentle rising and a slight disturbance throughout the moored fleet, as they rock more noisily and with more movement. But the tide soon goes out and the boats subside to their normal level once more. As they spend their days moored side by side, all they do is gather barnacles on the hull in a wasted existence.

Wouldn't it be thrilling if some of us would yield our hearts to Christ, and by His grace experience a growing maturity? Then, as He filled our hearts and lives, how exciting it would be to move into a sense of completeness in Him, to raise our sails, cast off the moorings, and move out unto the busy seas of life on business for the Master. How satisfying it would be to have every inch of canvas aloft, to sense the filling of the wind and the quiet driving of His Spirit. What a contrast to rocking in the church mooring!

> Also I heard the voice of the Lord, saying, Whom shall I send, and who will go for us? Then said I, Here am I; send me (Isaiah 6:8).

CHAPTER 12

LIMITING GOD THROUGH THE HOME

IN THE DAYS OF THE early Christian church as portrayed in the New Testament, the center of all the activity was the Christian home. Paul refers in I Corinthians 16:19 to Aquila and Priscilla, "with the church that is in their house." In Colossians 4:15 he greets Nymphas "and the church which is in his house." His letter to Philemon is addressed to Philemon, and to "Apphia, and Archippus our fellowsoldier, and the church in thy house."

In those days there were no sanctuaries or excellent church premises such as we have today, with buildings for Christian education. There were no Bibles or hymn books as we know them. But there was a tremendous power of effective witness and a dynamic outreach — all centered in, and radiating from, the Christian home.

One of the remarkable developments in the United States in recent years has been the rapid growth of Christian meetings held in private homes. These meetings seem to be springing up independently and almost "naturally," with no apparent human plan or organization behind them. Sometimes it is a special morning meeting for ladies where friends bring friends to meet around the Word of God. Some Christian women have been finding how easy it is to arrange such a meeting, how smoothly God seems to keep things moving, how the most unexpected women will come and — best of all — how many have come to meet and know the Lord Jesus as their own personal Saviour. In other homes it is a luncheon group or an evening group. Sometimes they listen to a special speaker or a message on a tape, or they study on their own. The ways are varied and the needs are tremendous, but it would seem that God has a definite work to do in the United States, and He is doing it once more through the Christian home. Many problems and difficulties emerge as the work goes on, and not all is as good as it might be, but the home is back once more as a means to an end in the hand of God.

Very often, however, the Christian home can be the one place where we limit God most. A study of the Bible will teach us how important the home is in the eyes of God. It is the unit with which He builds His church and His people. A reverse picture of the importance of the home can be seen in the way the Communists view it. Whereas God uses the home to build His people, the Communists seek to destroy the home as a family unit.

I was speaking sometime ago with a Chinese Christian who had come from Red China, and who had friends and relatives still there. He was fairly up to date on the state of the nation. I asked him what effect the Communists had had on his country. He replied that for the older people, it was another adverse outside influence. He explained that the basis of all previous Chinese culture was the home, the authority of the home, allegiance to the home, and a natural loyalty to all that the home and tradition stood for. To people raised in this older way of life, Communism was an inferior type of culture. "But," he went on, "when the Communists took over, they set about the systematic destruction of the home as a family unit." The younger generation were taught to despise the old ways and the old culture. They were encouraged to spy on parents and relations, and report acts that were contrary to the new laws of the land. Their allegiance was now to the state and the leader of the state. On such a generation the Communists now had a great hold and China as it used to be was being torn apart and rebuilt without the home. God builds the home and uses the home, but Communism destroys the home and all that it stands for.

In one area the American people are playing right into the hands of the Communists — in the ever-growing divorce rate. Statistics show that in the United States, one out of every four marriages ends in divorce. In California, this figure is one out of every three, and in Southern California official figures issued in San Bernardino in 1965 show that one out of every two marriages ends in divorce. In other words, the American people themselves are deliberately breaking up the home as a unit. This brings about a definite weakening in the moral and domestic fiber of the nation. Moreover it is giving the Communists exactly what they want — a people who are fast losing the meaning of the words love, loyalty and allegiance. With this gradual breakdown in the home life of the nation, it is all the more important that the Christian home should stand firm for all that is true and pure.

The importance of the home in the eyes of God is best seen in His arranging for the upbringing of His own Son. With all the world to choose from, and every home, rich and poor, at His command, our God chose the humble home in Nazareth as the place where the Lord Jesus should be raised. Not wealthy, not poverty-stricken — just a humble, hard-working, simple family home.

Did you ever wonder how many children Mary had besides her first-born Jesus? Matthew 13:55-57 tells us that the local people in Nazareth said about Jesus, "Is not this the carpenter's son? is not his mother called Mary? and his brethren, James, and Joses, and Simon, and Judas? And his sisters, are they not all with us?" We can learn from this that Mary had four more sons, all younger than Jesus. So Jesus had four half-brothers. The word *sisters* implies at least two, but the King James Version is wrong in the position of the word *all* in that phrase. Every other translation or version gives it "and all his sisters, are they not with us?" "His sisters" could mean two girls, but "all his sisters" means at least three. This gives us at least seven other children in the family besides Jesus, who was the oldest.

This is what God chose for His own Son — a family where there must have been problems and tensions, where the oldest boy would have plenty to do helping Joseph or Mary with the little ones. Consider also that Jesus stayed at home until He was thirty years old — a fact we so often overlook. Tradition says that Joseph died early, leaving Jesus as the man of the house.

There is another significant word in I Corinthians 9:5, where Paul says, "Have we not power to lead about a sister, a wife, as well as other apostles, and as the brethren of the Lord, and Cephas?" Scripture records that the four half-brothers of Jesus were married, so He had sisters-in-law as well — and probably brothers-in-law. As the other children married they would leave home. But Jesus stayed until He was thirty. Learn from this two things. First, God is so committed to the home and family as a unit, that His own Son took part, to the full, in such an experience. Second, when the Bible says in Hebrews 4:15 that Jesus was "in all points tempted [or tested] like as we are, yet without sin," it really means what it says. Jesus knew and experienced all the tensions and pressures of close family living.

Psalm 127 has much to teach us about the organization and development of a home, as prescribed by God Himself. We find here basic principles which are applicable to every age and national culture. The home which operates under these instructions is one in which God's will and purposes will be carried on. But the home which is simply following the pattern set by others in the community is in danger of failure and, above all, of limiting God.

The culture in which we live has developed a wrong emphasis with regard to marriage. The wedding ceremony, when the bridegroom and bride are united as husband and wife, is looked upon as the culmination of all that has gone before. All the glory and glamour are focused on the wedding day. At the end of the ceremony, there is a sense of completion — the whole thing is finally over. Now they are married, everyone can relax!

There is a sense in which this is true. A chapter has ended in the lives of these two. But the whole emphasis of Psalm 127 is that when the wedding is over, then the actual business of marriage really begins. It is this ignorance of what God says about the new relationship, that causes failure and weakness in so many Christian homes.

God has a pattern for each Christian home. The world has its own patterns for home-making and home-breaking. The tragedy is that so often we follow the patterns we see around us, and neglect God's pattern. Psalm 127 gives us definite guidance on *building* a home, *keeping* a home, *using* a home. If we allow the Word of God to speak to us, if we listen, and — most important — if we obey this teaching on the Christian home, then we can know with assurance that God is with us and our home will be to His honor and His glory.

Verse 1 gives us this instruction on building a home: "Except the Lord build the house, they labour in vain that build it." These few words challenge the basic structure of every Christian home today with their essential truth that there is only one Builder — God. In some homes the husband is the dynamic character. He does all the deciding and the planning and the arranging. In other Christian homes the wife has control. What she says decides the planning and running of the home. Most domestic tensions begin here. But the quiet resentments, the silent struggles for power, the clash of wills and personalities are the seeds of future breakdown.

All this is taken care of in verse 1: "Except the Lord build . . ." it is in vain. It is possible to have the most glamorous of weddings, and yet to find the married life an ever-increasing source of frustration, for that is what *in vain* can mean — frustration, with all its senseless struggle and waste of time, money and energy. There is only one Builder, only one who holds the blueprint and decides the detail and structure of the home. He knows the end from the beginning. He promises and guarantees blessing and success if we commit our times and our ways into His hands.

There is another half to this great truth in verse 1. There is only one Builder, but there must be two laborers. Here we can fail again in our building of a Christian home. God does the building, we do the laboring — but so many of us don't like being laborers! We would rather do the ordering and telling and let someone else do the hard work. The laboring can be physical, mental, or spiritual. It may involve a willingness to adjust, to submit, to give way. It often means going without, a willingness to sacrifice time and energy. Above all it includes a willingness to face reality and a determination not to shirk or avoid responsibility. These words sound good and pious. We all agree to them — on paper. But that isn't enough for God. He wants two laborers who are prepared to take orders from Him, and then work.

One point we often overlook is that God is always building. He is always on the move, always leading on to new plans and experiences. Because this is so, we must always be laboring. The only way to build a Christian home is to keep working at it. This is often where the first cracks appear in a Christian marriage. One member of the marriage either grows tired of laboring, or never really settles down to doing a real job of work, letting the load fall upon the other partner.

Recently I sat in on a very honest discussion where husbands and wives were sharing this very problem. It began because one of the men said that in the United States, the women ruled the home — what they said counted most and the husbands had to agree, or else! These words were said with much humor, but there was a gentle sense of resentment behind them.

Then one of the wives challenged the men. What else could they expect? The men shirked their jobs in the home, they left the raising of the children to the mother, they forced the wife to make the decisions. Whose fault was it?

As they continued their discussion, each side added more evidence to the initial points just stated. All that they said was true. These things did happen. Some husbands did go off and leave their wives to cope with the domestic situation. Some wives were slack in their home responsibilities. Everything they said proved the truth of Psalm 127:1: "Except the Lord build . . . they labor in vain." God, the only Builder, is constantly at work, and we must be willing laborers who are constantly prepared to work also. If we fail in our part, then God is limited in the Christian home.

I spend much time in counseling with husbands and wives. As a result I have noticed one area in particular in the marriage relationship which is always in need of "laboring." I can illustrate this best in the words spoken to me this past summer by a wife in her early fifties. "My husband is good and kind, he is a very good father to our children. But in recent years he simply takes me for granted. I feel like a piece of mobile furniture. He never says the lovely things he used to say. I feel so unloved and lonely."

When I spoke to the husband, I asked him if he loved his wife. He looked most surprised and replied, "Of course

I love her, why do you think I married her?" But he said it in such a way that it sounded dry and colorless and uninteresting.

Since then I have felt burdened to speak to men about the subject of the Christian home, to urge them to consider their marriage relationship most earnestly. As the years go by, the wife may not be as lovely and attractive as she used to be. The tendency is to allow the affections to become, likewise, less lovely and less attractive. But it is especially then that she needs all the more love and kindness and tender affection. Here is an area where there needs to be some real heart-searching, and where we need to work at it. Laboring isn't always doing physical work. It is often making mental and spiritual adjustments and readjustments.

Wives also need to remember that this is equally as real and necessary in their attitude to their husbands. As the years go by the husband ceases to be the young, athletic character who first attracted them. Age slows him down and fills him out. But it is just then that he needs the extra love and admiration and the tender, willing sympathy of the only one who can truly understand him. Every man is still a boy at heart, and every wife should know this, and respond accordingly. In both cases, the blessing only comes when we are prepared to take time to keep on laboring while God is still building.

Before we leave this subject of building a home we need to be sure that I Corinthians 3:9-15 means something real in our experience. Verse 9 says that "we are laborers together with God." I know this has a specific reference to Paul and his ministry, but the truth is also applicable to the Christian home. Verse 10 says, "But let every man take heed how he buildeth thereupon." Notice how personal this is, the words "every man" occur six times in these few verses. Verse 11 speaks of the foundation of the Christian home: "For other foundation can no man lay than that is laid, which is Jesus

Christ." The foundation is the person of Christ, not merely the work of Christ. It isn't enough to know that Jesus Christ died for me on the cross. As we have seen in this book already, God's answer to our need is the risen Christ who lives in us through His Holy Spirit. He is the Builder, and by His presence in our hearts and homes, the Christian home becomes a living reality.

Notice also the solemn fact that "every man's work shall be made manifest: for the day shall declare it" (verse 13). Some day I will have to give an account to God of my work as a laborer in my own home. The following words also challenge us: "the fire shall try every man's work of what sort it is." Notice that the work is not tested for *how much* it is, but for *what sort* it is.

These verses in I Corinthians speak primarily of the responsibilities of a Christian in working and witnessing for God in the world as a whole. But we must remember that the greatest witness for Christ in the world today is a truly Christian home where God is honored, and His Word obeyed. The test therefore in verse 13 is "of what sort it is." The success of my home is not the size of it, nor the bank balance behind it, nor the number of cars and "things" in it. God looks for one thing only: what kind it is, whether His building has been matched by our laboring, whether His plans are the product shown in our home.

Psalm 127 goes on to tell us that

except the Lord keep the city, the watchman waketh but in vain. It is vain for you to rise up early, to sit up late, to eat the bread of sorrows: for so he giveth his beloved sleep.

Here the Word of God teaches us how to *keep* the home. Notice immediately the similarity between the building and the keeping of the home. "Except the Lord build . . . *except the Lord keep* . . ." Just as there is one Builder, so there is one Keeper — God.

How true are the words of verse 2: "It is vain for you to rise up early, to sit up late, to eat the bread of sorrows." I have come across several Christian homes where parents rise up early, and sit up late, and eat the bread of sorrows — wondering what their children are doing, where they are and what will happen when they come home — if they come home. The ways of God are past finding out, and in some cases the finest godly homes are beset with the problem of wayward children. Many cases, however, which have come to my attention are the result of the failure of the parents to obey the Word of God — either through ignorance or laziness. What can one say to a mother who comes with the pathetic outburst, "My daughter is a teenager next week. What can I do about it?" Not all remarks are as naive as that, but there is an attitude of mind which avoids taking any deliberate action with growing children, apparently hoping that the children will sort themselves out. This attitude is never the teaching of the Bible which exhorts parents to train up a child in the way he should go, to use discipline, to exert authority and to expect respect.

A closer look into verse 1 — "except the Lord keep the city, the watchman waketh but in vain" — shows us that there is one keeper, who is the Lord, and one watchman (not the watchwoman or watchparents, but watchman). This is God's order and truth, but a truth which is being constantly overlooked and neglected. God's plan for a Christian home is that the husband, not the wife, is the watchman.

The word watchman has the idea of a sentry — someone who is always on guard. The watchman's job is to watch, not to fight. In war when the sentry stands watch, his job is to be constantly alert and responsive. If he recognizes an enemy approaching, he doesn't go out and fight by himself. His job is to give the warning so that there can be an effective resistance made by the forces on his side. His job is to watch and warn.

This is exactly the teaching of this verse. The watchman does not fight — God's responsibility is to keep the city. The watchman's job is to bring the power of God to bear on a particular circumstance or situation. In the family this is the task of the husband and father. He will be on guard as his children grow, watching that which comes into the home — friends, literature, TV programs, outside influences — everything which can shape or mar human character. This is his responsibility, not the mother's.

It is at this point where there is a lack in many homes. Either the watching is left to the mother, or the job is quietly avoided. To follow the standards set by non-Christian homes in the community is to ask for future trouble. The easiest way at the time is to do nothing about it — to send the watchman off duty and hope for the best. But this is where verse 2 comes in. "It is vain [absolutely useless] for you to rise up early, to sit up late, to eat the bread of sorrows." Neglect of training and guarding and watching while the children are young will reap a harvest of trouble when they are teenagers.

The watchman's job is to call out the power to protect. When the father recognizes the need and the danger, he should come, with the mother, in earnest prayer to God, seeking wisdom as to what action should be taken, committing the problem to the Lord and taking that necessary action. One sure way of keeping watch is to be constant and regular with the family altar. Let the children take part in the prayers and reading. If they are tiny, the time spent in devotions will be short but to the point, and always practical. Growing children can join in more and more. Part of the devotion time will be, at times, training in recognizing "the enemy." In this way the watchman will have his people ready to respond to any danger that he may recognize.

It should be a warning and an encouragement to every father to read Ezekiel 33:1-7. Here are detailed the duties and responsibilities of the watchman, especially in verse 6:

> But if the watchman see the sword come, and blow not the trumpet, and the people be not warned; if the sword come, and take any person from among them, he is taken in his iniquity; but his blood will I require at the watchman's hands.

What searching words these are, especially when we put them alongside the words we found in I Corinthians 3:13, "Every man's work shall be manifest . . . of what sort it is."

Every father has to answer to God for the way he has watched and guided his children. This is one of the great responsibilities of parenthood. But I can think of some Christian fathers who are doing exactly nothing to watch and guard their children. We need to remember that the example we set before our children is going to be a subject for discussion when we appear before Christ at His judgment seat.

We have thought of *building* a home, and of *keeping* a home. The final section of Psalm 127 concerns *using* a home. The sequence of thought here is interesting — God keeps that which He builds, and uses that which He keeps.

Verse 3 tells us that "children are an heritage of the Lord." This thought needs careful consideration and follows directly from our previous thoughts about the duties and responsibilities of the watchman. Our children are not temporary guests in our home, for whom we care but for whom we have no real lasting consideration. They are an inheritance from the Lord. God has an infinite interest in our children. They were His before they became ours. It is our duty and responsibility to invest time and energy in them — not to exploit them as "live" toys provided for our pleasure. As we have seen, as parents we will have to answer some day for the results of our parenthood, and the outcome of our training.

Verse 4 has a lovely thought for the truly Christian home: "As arrows are in the hand of a mighty man; so are children of the youth." Children are as arrows, not as a sword. The idea here is that the arrow can go where the mighty man cannot reach. This is true of many a Christian home.

I remember recently being in the home of a fine Christian couple. They showed me the pictures of their five children. All were now grown up. Three were medical doctors, one was a minister and one was a nurse. Three of the children were overseas on the mission field. What a lovely family — five arrows that had been sent forth out of that home. They had all gone where the parents could not reach! God had built that home, God had kept that home, and now He was using it. But all this did not happen by chance. Over the years there had been much "blood, toil, tears and sweat" — but in the hands of God, and through the outworking of His Holy Spirit.

Verse 5 ends with a happy expression: "they shall not be ashamed, but they shall speak with the enemies in the gate." The original text does not specify who the "they" are. It could be either the parents or the children, or both. The parents won't be ashamed of the children, and the children won't be ashamed of the parents — if God has built and kept and used the home. As a final result "they shall speak with [or subdue and destroy] the enemies in the gate." There will be victory for Christ, honor and glory for Christ. It will come because of two laborers who kept on working, because of one watchman who continued watching and warning, because of two parents who were mindful of their responsibility, and who invested time and love and patience in their children.

This is God's picture and pattern for the normal Christian home. Inasmuch as we choose to follow another pattern, then in that much we limit God in our own home. But following God's pattern will be rewarding, satisfying, and productive of untold blessing in the days to come.

THE ZONDERVAN PAPERBACK SERIES
96 pages each, 69c
THE POWER OF POSITIVE PRAYING — John Bisagno   No. 9238s

THE REBELLIOUS PLANET — Lon Woodrum   No. 12292s

YOU CAN WITNESS WITH CONFIDENCE — Rosalind Rinker
   No. 10714s

APOSTLE TO THE ILLITERATES (Frank C. Laubach)—David Mason
   No. 10141s

THE GOSPEL BLIMP — Joe Bayly   No. 12288s

FREEDOM FROM THE SEVEN DEADLY SINS — Billy Graham
   No. 9716s

128 pages each, 79c
A BIT OF HONEY (After-dinner speeches) — W. E. Thorn
   No. 10928s

PLAY BALL! — James Hefley   No. 9797s

PRAYER — CONVERSING WITH GOD — Rosalind Rinker
   No. 10716s

HOW TO ENJOY THE CHRISTIAN LIFE—Don Mainprize   No. 10106s

THESE MY PEOPLE — Lillian Dickson   No. 9524s

LIFE IS FOR LIVING — Betty Carlson   No. 9384s

SCIENCE RETURNS TO GOD — James H. Jauncey   No. 9927s

NEVER A DULL MOMENT — Eugenia Price   No. 10584s

THE BIBLE FOR TODAY'S WORLD — W. A. Criswell   No. 9426s

160 pages each, 89c
ABOVE OURSELVES — James H. Jauncey   No. 9950s

BECOMING A CHRISTIAN — Rosalind Rinker   No. 10718s

BUT GOD! — V. Raymond Edman   No. 9595s

FIND OUT FOR YOURSELF — Eugenia Price   No. 10603s

LIVING CAN BE EXCITING — Aaron N. Meckel   No. 12280s

THE SAVING LIFE OF CHRIST — W. Ian Thomas   No. 10980s

YOUR CHILD — Anna B. Mow   No. 12256s

SAY 'YES' TO LIFE — Anna B. Mow   No. 10383s

KNOWING GOD'S SECRETS — John Hunter   No. 9883s

THEY FOUND THE SECRET — V. Raymond Edman   No. 9564s

WE'RE NEVER ALONE — Eileen Guder   No. 9710s

MAN TO MAN — Richard C. Halverson   No. 6818s

LIMITING GOD — John Hunter   No. 4702s

192 pages each, 98c
A WOMAN'S WORLD — Clyde Narramore   No. 12230s

HELLBENT FOR ELECTION — P. Speshock   No. 10830s

LIFE AND LOVE — Clyde Narramore   No. 10412s

YOUNG ONLY ONCE — Clyde Narramore   No. 10414s

HOW TO WIN OVER WORRY — John Haggai   No. 9740s

GAMES FOR ALL OCCASIONS — Carlson and Anderson   No. 9051s

Approximately 256 pages each, 98c
WOMAN TO WOMAN — Eugenia Price   No. 10589s

PILGRIM'S PROGRESS — John Bunyan   No. 6610s

LET MY HEART BE BROKEN — Richard Gehman   No. 9694s